River of Life

Sister Mary J. Steinkamp, SNJM

Sister Mary J. Steinkamp

LC LONGWOOD
COMMUNICATIONS

Cover Design;
Cheryl M. Gower
gowergraphics
Gervais, OR

Printed in the United States of America

International Standard Book Number: 1-883928-14-1

Library of Congress Catalog Card Number: 95-079831

Drawings by Sister Helen Moore, SNJM

and Sister Mary J. Steinkamp, SNJM

Photos by Zita Steinkamp

Published by:

Longwood Communications

397 Kingslake Drive

DeBary, Florida 32713

904-774-1991

To contact the author:

Sister Mary J. Steinkamp, SNJM

605 Seventh Street

Box 215

Gervais, OR 97026

503-792-3202

RIVER OF LIFE

Contents

Detailed Chapter Outline

Dedication

I dedicate
> this book to Mary,
>> Mother of Jesus,
>> Smile of the Spirit,
>> Joy of the Father,
and the Peace that surrounds the Trinity.

Introduction

God Helped me through many friends in the charismatic movement. He showed me in a thirty-day retreat how all encompassing His love is.

He Told me, "I am your River of Life. Swim deliciously free in me." It is a powerful message, one that I feel compelled to share.

I pray that many will come to know how deep and high and strong God's love is through reading and praying this reflection book.

Chapter 1 River of Life

River of Life

"The angel then showed me the river of life-giving water, clear as crystal, which issued from the throne of God and of the lamb and flowed down the middle of the street. On either side of the river grew the trees of life which produce fruit twelve times a year... their leaves serve as medicine for the nations."   *Rev. 22:1-2*

"It is he who gives . . . life and breath and everything else."
Acts 17:25

And Jesus spoke:

My child,

My love is a river,

ever flowing through your life.

My love is clear as crystal.

My love focuses everything for you.

Look with my eyes of love and you will see as I do.

My Love is my Spirit flowing through your life.

My River of Life produces much fruit.

It nourishes trees of peace,

of hope,

of neighborliness,

of justice,

of kindness,

of generosity.
My River of Life can unify hearts and nations
                if it is allowed to do so.
Make every effort to preserve the unity
                which has my Spirit as its origin
                and peace as its binding force.

Begin with yourself.
In me all things are possible.
In me the difficult is smooth.
In me the stubborn is docile.
In me the icy melts.
In me truth and hope and joy flow
                like unending rivers.
        Give me yourself in as many ways
                as your imagination paints.
Give me yourself peacefully,
        lovingly,
        hopefully,
        quietly,
        trustingly,
        rambunctiously,
        joyfully.
Give me yourself in storms at sea,
        in low tide,
        in high tide,

in rushing waters,

in peaceful calms.

You do not see—let me be your eyes.

You do not understand—let me be your understanding.

You do not know—let me be your knowledge.

Trust me with every care that weighs you down

and I will bless you.

Come to me day and night and you will know

Life,

Love,

Truth,

Goodness.

All things will be at peace in you

because you will be in me.

To find me is to find life and nothing else matters.

I am your River of Life,

Swim deliciously free in me.

Chapter 2
Desert

And the desert shall rejoice, and blossom as a rose

Is. 35:1 (KJV)

5

Filling the Desert

". . . the desert and the parched land will exalt... they will bloom with abundant flowers and rejoice with joyful song." *Is. 35:1*

" I will open up rivers on the bare heights, and fountains in the broad valleys; I will turn the desert into a marshland, and the dry ground into springs of water." *Is. 41:18*

> The single rose
> Is now the garden
> Where all loves end
> Terminate torment
> Of love unsatisfied.
>
> *(Ash Wednesday, T.S. Eliot)*

It was a desert year. I had been missioned to an outlying school that held no attraction for me. My friends were in the big city. The liturgies were pre-Trent and barren. The place was isolated. I had no car or driver's license. Truly I felt as if I were in a desert. Yet Jesus never let me down:

My child, I will free you from yourself.

I will love you with a love as big as God Himself.

I will pick you up and put you back together.

Have no fears.

Rest in my arms.

Let my love run freely through you.

You belong to me.

Nothing else matters.

My peace can heal all that is hurting in you.

My tender forgiveness can untangle the most tangled

skeins of human relationships.

I know you seek me with all your heart.

Have no fear.

Trust with a loving heart.

Open your hands and let the nails of today in.

In pain you will grow in my love,

In pain you will know me with a freedom not found on
        this earth.

Do not shrink from pain for I am there.

My love is bigger than all the pain this world can offer.

My love will support you.

I am with you even when you feel nothing,

When your heart cries out for human companionship

When you know nothing but aridity and desolation.

I am with you.

I have traveled the desert.

I have brought the Living Water.

The Desert of Nothingness

"I will not leave you orphaned; I will come back to you."

John 14:18

Walk where my love will take you.

Do not stumble, do not hesitate, do not turn back.

I am with you.

Trust me, little one.

Look up and let me see you smile as you give me your
      nothingness.

I love you.

I do not ask for brave deeds or big wonders;

I want only you.

The love of your heart is all I seek.

Do not run away.

Fall into my arms and let my gentle peace smooth away
      all your cares.

Give me your nothingness.

It is the best gift you can give.

Wrap it in the paper of my mercy and tie it with the
      bow of my love.

Then give it right from your heart and my heart will
      receive it warmly.

Desert Fruitfulness

O my beloved,
I will lure you into the desert
Where my spirit will speak to your heart.
I will strip you of all things—
    Naked,
    You will stand before me,
    Clad only
    In the vesture
    Of my love.
I will place you on the cross,
    And you will cry out,
But my love will support you,
And I will show you the way to the Father,
    Where together
    We will join
    That full circle of praise,
    My Trinity.

Faith in Darkness

"Do not let your hearts be troubled. Have faith in God, and
have faith in me."
John 14:1

Walk with me.

Talk to me.

See me in all that is and will be.

Trust your sick mother to me—

I see her needs, I hear her cries, I am answering.

Do not let your heart be troubled.

I am carrying all your cares in my heart.

Trust me.

Give up your own ideas on how things should go.

Let me be Lord of your life.

Abandon yourself to me—

I am your answer, I am your stillpoint,

I am the true center of your being.

Trust me with all your heart,

And you will know new life,

You will know new hope.

The things that weigh you down will disappear.

In me you will find what you seek—

      Oneness,

      peace,

freedom
the effervescence of living,
the sparkle that comes
from the joy of my Spirit in you.
Praise and peace will flow,
And you will know that it is my doing,
not yours.

Faith

"Blest are they who have not seen, and have believed."

John 20:29

Sit still and let me speak in the quiet recesses of your heart.

I am calling you to be a hope-builder,

I am calling you to have faith in my ability to work through
your weakness.

Think about the lady who touched the hem of my garment.

She believed and my power went through her.

Consider the centurion whose son lay sick.

He believed and my power healed his son.

Remember Peter on the water

When he kept his eyes on me,

all went well.

Reflect on the man who was blind.

He cried, "Lord, that I may see." He had faith and saw.

If you have faith you will see me.

Each day you will see more of me.

Each day your eyes will behold my power in new and
deeper ways.

I am with you.

You do not need to know any more right now.

I will guide you, I am your light.

Trim your lamp of faith and come closer.

I am manifest in the sunset,
    in the wind,
    in the trees,
in the fat robins,
in the chattering children,
    in the serious adults,
    in flowing water,
    in my Mother's caring ways.
Yes, I am with you.
Open your eyes of faith and see!

*I am manifest
in chattering children*

Wasteland

Is. 32:9-20

Dear hard-headed one,

Go into my desert and learn who you are.

Feel the hot wind blowing.

Taste the dryness.

Smell the acrid sands.

Strip yourself of all that stands between you and me.

See your nothingness and let me fill it.

I long to gather you into my arms and let you know the full
ness of my Father's love.

I long to heal the scars that are upon you from the past.

I long to let my light shine through these scars.

Come aside and do not be troubled at the sight of my desert.

Be aware that I first met the Spirit in the desert.

Know, O hard-headed one, that there is room for my Spirit to
get in.

Washed in tears, stand before me ready to be filled.

Do not be afraid of your own nothingness;

It is my ticket for entry,

It is my way of claiming you for my own.

I fill those who come open and ready to be filled.

I fill those who are empty of clutter, that my spirit may have
room to breathe.

Child of pain, child of struggle, let me live in you.

Trust me to do in you all that needs to be done.

Do not hurry; do not fret; do not try so hard.

I am doing all things by the power of my Spirit in the timing of my Father.

Be at peace. Be at ease.

The wasteland of your heart is being made fertile by the power of my Spirit.

All those things that to you seem lost are being restored by the power of my spirit.

The old is falling away and the desert is becoming an oasis of my spirit's delights.

Drink deeply and know life.

Have confidence in the way my Spirit works in you.

My ways are not your ways; my thoughts are not your thoughts.

I do all things in the will of Him who sent me.

Listen to my Spirit in you and you will have no trouble following the will of my Father in this wasteland.

The Fullness of Emptiness

Jesus was led into the desert where He met the Spirit.

Beloved sprout of the Father,

I have called you to loving faithfulness.

My love in you has not been void.

Give me your heart as you did 37 years ago.

Let me keep it close to the Father.

Trust me to act in you.

Commit your life daily to me and I will act.

Trust me to do in you all that needs doing.

I am the Master Pruner.

I am the Master Lover.

My love will fashion you for the Father.

Do not be afraid of the process,
> for your heart has to be hollowed out
> to receive all I have to give.

>> You are my reed;
>>> you must be empty for the tune.

>> You are my cup;
>>> you must be empty for my wine.

>> You are my river bed;
>>> I am your living water.

>> You must be hollowed out to receive me.

>> I must dredge you deep
>>> that my Spirit might run free within you.

Step back from the fear of emptiness and
    let my love fill you, transform you.

Look back and see how my love has guided you
    from the day you gave me your heart.

Trust me to continue to fashion you
    in my love and praise and never stop giving.

I am your source of giving, I am your fountain
    that never runs dry.

I am a river that flows forever in the freedom
    of the Spirit and the great kindness of the Father.

Know our Trinitarian love and you will know life.

Love, and you will give life.

Praise, and you will regenerate the earth.

Chapter 3 Trust

I come to
you in
little ways

a perfect
maple leaf,

a yellow
cowslip.

Trust

"Wait for the LORD with courage;
Be stouthearted, and wait for the LORD."   *Ps. 27:14*

I felt discouraged and down because four youngsters in a class of thirty were raising havoc. I felt even more down when I remembered how a classroom minority had wrecked the majority. Fear paralyzed me. I was afraid of my own inabilities. I turned to the Lord. His answer was:

Do not squirm so; I am with you.

I will never drop you.

My love and goodness flow through your life
         like unending rivers.

Trust me. Look to me and live.

Turn everything over to me

and don't sneak little worry bits.

I am big enough, strong enough,
         loving enough to handle everything.

Why do you doubt, O you of little faith?

Come to me and I will refresh you.

My kindness is better than life.

I have loved you with an everlasting love;

Therefore have I drawn you, taking compassion on you.

My love is bigger than the ocean

         higher than the sky,

         deeper than Aristotle,

more beautiful than a rose,

fuller than a starry sky.

I do not need all your activities.

All I ask is your love. Give me your heart.

Let me fill you with all that is good

and beautiful

and true.

Let me wash away your preoccupation with the past,

your digging up of dry bones,

your uncorking of past resentments, failures.

I can wash you clean. I will wash you clean.

I will give you a new heart and make you a new person.

I will give you confidence in your work.

O my beloved, you are mine, I seek your heart.

I delight in your love! I do not look at your weakness.

*Stoop to me in the
lowly daisy*

*Admire me
in the
mighty oak.*

The Spirit of Jesus

"See! I will bring my Spirit into you, that you may come to life."

Ezek. 37:5

My little one without much hope,

I come to you as morning rain,

gently,

quietly,

falling on your heart,

washing away your worries,

picking you up

and putting the jagged pieces together.

My child, I love you,

I will never abandon you.

I go before you always,

My Presence is with you.

Let my goodness fill you and drive out all your fears.

Tension in not of me,

I come in peace.

My message is PEACE,

My heart is full of peace.

I desire peace for you.

Know me in the peace of all creation.

Find me in the rose.

Touch me in the vibrant walnut tree.

Love me in the jade plant,

Admire me in the mighty oak,

Stoop to me in the lowly daisy.

Know the wonder of my love in all creation.

I am being poured out like a libation--receive me.

I seek you with all my heart;

I want you;

I desire all your fears and stacked-up worries.

Give them to me and know the peace that runs over.

Let go for you will not find me in hanging on.

Your heart will be torn and divided and too concerned
about mundane things.

Do not be troubled about what you eat and wear.

Look at the lilies of the field.

Does not my Father clothe them?

Look at the birds of the air.

Do they ever go hungry?

Why do you fret? Why do you hassle? Come to me.

Lay aside all these hassles.

I am a gentle stream of peace

Not bound by tension and struggle.

I come in the gentle wind;

No hurricanes for me.

I come in a quiet flame;

No blazing uproar for me.

Know me in peace and in the stillness of your own heart.

I love you and I would not have you expend yourself in
needless worry.

Rest in the hope that springs eternal

From my Father's life-giving Spirit.

Letting Go of Fear

"I sought the LORD, and he answered me,
and delivered me from all my fears."   *Ps. 34:4*

My child of heavy concerns,

I see your fumbling hands.

I hear your labored breathing.

I feel your heavy heart.

Do not run away from your fears;

Give them to me.

Seek me with all your heart

and you will find me.

Come to me and let my love

   heal all that is undone

   and aching in you.

Let not your heart be troubled nor let it be afraid;

You believe in God, believe also in me.

Give me those things that burned your heart.

Let me restore your hope.

Be true to my word and my word will be true to you.

   My word is life.

   My word is hope.

   My word is strength.

   My word is power.

Let my word empower you.

You cannot do it alone.

Come to me and I will refresh you.

I will wash away your cares;

I will show you the path of peace.

In my will is perfect peace.

Have faith and follow my word
written in your heart.

My Father and I are one in that great sea of love
which is the Spirit.

You must be one with us.

You must learn to let our love fill every pore,
every crevice,
every crack of your being.
Love pushes out fear.

When you love with all your being, you will know
only our guiding hand.

Come and know the peace my Father has in store
for those who love him.

Relinquish that burden of fear,
that tight wad of worry;

Give it to me and I will give you the good things
of my Father—peace, hope, joy.

Walk with me and know the strength of living
in our Trinity

Openness

"The seed on good ground are those who hear the word in a spirit of openness, retain it, and bear fruit through perserverance."

Luke 8:15

My child,

I come to you in the night.

I come to remove your fears.

I fill you with love.

I take away in you anything
       that pulls you away form reality,
       for I am reality.

I am for you the most real person there is.

       Do not doubt.

       Do not hesitate.

       Do not be afraid.

I am light, and love, and laughter.

I will fill you, but first you must be open
       and ask for me.

You must be willing to let go
       of all your petty concerns.

You must have the freedom to let me in.

You must open your door wide and
       stop peeking through the crack.

You must open your arms and let me in as only you can.

Behold, I come gently.

I come quietly.

I come only when I'm asked.

I come bearing gifts, the very gifts you need

to live in me—

love,

joy,

patience,

hope,

and an abiding trust.

I desire that you come to me joyously,

praising the Father,

glorifying my Trinity,

imitating my Mother.

Bask in my love, for my love has hold of you
and will carry you to the Father.

Union
with me
will show
you new
beauty
in every
atom of
creation

God's Ways

"For my thoughts are not your thoughts, nor
are your ways my ways, says the LORD."   *Is. 55:8*

You seek me and I want to respond.

I do not answer you in the ways you expect.

Be open to my coming for it is

      as gentle as the breeze,

      as imperceptible as the clouds,

      as loving as Mary,

      and as all-encompassing as my Spirit.

I come to you daily—watch at my door posts.

Hear instruction—be wise and refuse it not.

I am closer to you than your own heartbeat.

Recognize me and love me with all your might.

Know my peace and merciful forgiveness.

Open your whole being to the wonder of my love.

I am with you down the nights and down the days.

Like the rain that comes down and waters the earth
      and does not return void.

So my Word comes down and fills your heart
      and does not return to the Father void.

My love for you is freely given—

Likewise must yours be.

Freely share the love I have poured into you.

Like an unending river my love for you flows on,

Like a mighty well that never goes dry,

Like an ocean, mighty and deep,
  my love inundates you.

Let my love deepen my Presence in you.

Let my love catch you up and carry you to the Father.

Let my love teach you joy in all things, even pain.

Live in me as I do in you.

My heart thirsts for your love;

I desire to be one with you.

Renew your covenant with me daily.

Accept lovingly everything from the hand of my Father,
  as I did in the garden.

Know the peace of uniting your will with mine.

My child, I desire union.

Union with me will free you to be your best self.

Union with me will show you a new beauty
  in every atom of creation.

Union with me will expand your heart to praise me
  in everything that happens to you.

Every pain, every sorrow, every joy, every tear
  is my gift to you.

It is lovingly given that you might come to the Father
  on the wings of my Spirit.

I come to you in little
ways, a flowering
                dogwood,

My hope is seen in a tiny blossom.

Finding the God of Hope

In Him we live and breathe and have our being . . .

Let go of your own image, and you will find my image.
Let go of what binds you to worry and fear—I am in neither.
I am not in the howling wind that crushed the rocks,
Nor in the giant earthquake that tore the mountain asunder,
Nor in the raging fire that destroyed all in its path.
I come in a gentle breeze—

> tiny,

> whispering,

> unobtrusive.

I come to you in little ways—

> a flowering dogwood,

> a yellow cowslip,

> a perfect maple leaf.

Do not be sad—I am with you.
I give you my words, I speak to your heart.
I encourage you to help others.
Give me your worry and doubt for I desire your whole being.
Trust me to do in you all that needs to be done.
I am a loving God—I come to you gently, peacefully,
    hopefully.
I build up–I never tear down.
When you feel torn down, be assured it's not of me.

I am a God of Hope.

I bring new hope to a world that needs hope
      more than ever
      in the history of my people.

My hope is seen in a tiny blossom.

Find it there and share it.

Letting Go

"Trust in the LORD with all your heart,
on your own intelligence rely not."   *Prov. 3:5*

Let my Spirit in you guide you.

Let me possess you.

Let go of all your petty insecurities.

Let my Mother teach you the art of surrender,
    of total giving.

Trust me with all your heart.

Pray for trust and openness
    and a non-judgmental attitude.

Mend your own fences and do not count the holes
    in your neighbor's fences.

Live in the power of my love
    and my gifts in you will be fruitful.

I desire to heal my people.

You will be an instrument of healing.

You will be a channel of my love.

You will be fruitful
    as long as you are connected to me,
    as long as you let go of all else,
    as long as you let my river of life
    flow through you.

Come to the water, stand by my side.

I know you are thirsty, you won't be denied.

On either side of this river of life

Are growing trees of faith and fruitfulness.

Use that fruit to feed my people.

Drink deeply of my river of life

     and you will know me in every event,

         in every wild iris,

         in every situation.

You will praise me in laughter and sunshine.

You will know me with a joy not of this earth.

Come, O daughter, come without paying,
    come without cost.

Come let me love life into you, the very life I wish you to
    share.

*There is no forest
so black my light
can't penetrate it.*

Eyes on God

"The people who walked in darkness have seen a great light..."

> Pouring out a thousand graces,
> He passed these groves in haste;
> And having looked at them,
> With His image alone
> Clothed them in His beauty.

St. John of the Cross

They asked me to give a talk on the techniques of using murals as a teaching device at a state-wide reading meeting. I agreed to do it, knowing that public speaking was not my gift. My friend, Sister Arlene, came to support me. About ten teachers drifted in for my presentation and four walked out in the middle. Although I had spent hours preparing my talk, I felt it was a failure. I felt very down. I needed perspective. It is difficult to keep focused on the Lord. It is a real blessing to let Him clothe me with His beauty and for me to take my eyes off my own failures.

O, my beloved,

I do love you.

I have loved you even when you don't feel too
    great, physically or emotionally.

I will guide you.

I will lead you.

Trust me.

Do not look to things and people. My love will sustain you.

Walk peacefully in my ways of trust.

There is no door so big I can't open it.

There is no problem so large I can't tackle it.

There is no forest so black my light can't
       penetrate it.

Look to me with love and confidence.

I am with you.

I live in you.

My love pulses through your veins.

Trust me with a loving heart
       and you will know me
       in the blackest night.

I will focus your eyes on true values

I will turn you toward my Father and
       He will give you the perspective
       you need to see
       through the darkness.

Acceptance

Love is patient; love is kind. Love is not jealous, it does not put on airs, it is not snobbish. Love is never rude, it is not self-seeking, it is not prone to anger; neither does it brood over injuries. Love does not rejoice in what is wrong but rejoices with the truth. There is no limit to love's forbearance, to its trust, its hope, its power to endure.
1 Cor. 13:4-7

My child,
This is the fortification I ask of you

Do not explain.
Do not excuse.
Do not quibble.
Do not trump up reasons.

Accept everything as coming from my hand.

Accept.
Accept.
Accept.

Yes, I understand—

when you feel totally abandoned
by someone you love,
it is much harder.

You must learn to lean on me.
Seek me with all your heart.

Accept what is pulling you apart
And understand I ask this of you
because I love you.

Give me your love
unquestioningly,
fully,
completely,
without a hassle.

Prayer

"Never cease praying, render constant thanks,

such is God's will for you in Christ Jesus."   *1 Thess. 5:17,18*

"You will receive all that you pray for,

provided you have faith."   *Matt. 21:22*

I wanted the children's program to go perfectly, so I rehearsed the sixth grade until they were weary. Then, when several forgot their lines and the singing was anemic, I was upset.

Why God? Why was it such a flop? Why didn't you let it succeed? God as much as told me, "Your heart was not made for programs. Your heart was made for me. Listen." I listened.

Your heart was made for praying.

You will know no peace

until your spirit is one with mine.

Pray in-between.

Stop thinking you have to have quiet time

Use the time I give you.

Pray when you are working.

Pray when you are walking.

Pray when you balance the checkbook.

Pray when you supervise the children.

Pray when you eat and when you sleep.

Ask my Spirit in you to pray when you sleep. He will. Your heart was made for prayer and nothing else can satisfy it.

You hunger for me with a hunger
>   not known on this earth.
Wake up and realize I put that hunger there.

My Spirit in you calls out, "Abba, Father."
My Spirit in you strives constantly
>   for complete union with the Father.
Let that union take place.
Cooperate with all your heart and soul
>   and mind and will.
Give and never stop giving.
Ask your friend to help you
>   for she knows the Father and the Father knows her.

Continue in all I have asked you to do.
But above all, give me your emotions.
It won't happen overnight, but keep on trying.
When you least feel me, I am most there.
If you could but begin to realize
HOW MUCH I LOVE YOU!

Lift up your heart and fall into my arms.
All is peace there
>   and complete giving is total fulfillment of love.

Jesus Tells of His Spirit

"Not by an army, nor by might,
but by my spirit, says the LORD of hosts."   *Zach. 4:6*

Feel the whisper of my Spirit in the depths of your soul. Know the gentle stirring of my love in the quiet stillness
of your heart.
I come quietly.
I come gently.
You will know me in the soft breeze.
You will feel me in the warm sunshine
in the maple leaves.
You will embrace me in the quiet stillness
of the evening.
My Spirit speaks in the depths of your heart.
My Spirit carries you ever so quietly, ever so swiftly,
ever so peacefully to the Father.
My Spirit knows your needs and brings them
ever so powerfully to the Father.
My Spirit pleads for you as no one else can.

Trust all to Him.
He is ever active, ever new,
ever renewing, ever refreshing,
ever delightful in His love.

48

Let that love so immerse you that nothing on earth
can matter but me.

Open wide your arms and let me fill you with my Spirit.
Let truth and patience,
joy and benignity,
long-suffering and hope,
peace and fortitude,
faith and love,
All that is my Spirit
fill you,
for I have come that you may have life
and may have it to the full.
What will I but that you be filled?
If you did but know the gift! and Him who sent it!
O my child, if you could but comprehend what it means
to be filled with my Spirit!
If you did but know the fullness of God!
If you could but grasp the height and depth and width
of my love!

Trust in god

"The favors of the LORD are not exhausted,

his mercies are not spent;

They are renewed each morning

so great is his faithfulness."   *Lam. 3:22-26*

Do not squirm so.

Trust me.

I am with you.

Peace is my best gift to you.

I long to fill you with myself.

Stop struggling and let go of all the things
        you insist on cluttering up your mind with.

My goodness will follow you all the days of your life.

Live this moment in your love.

Leave yesterday to my mercy
        and tomorrow to my providence.

I am your God.

I am unlimited, unshackled by mundane considerations.

When your high school closed, I asked you to give me
        your heart and not to worry about all those other
        loose ends.

All that is necessary is that you BE IN ME.
Rest in my love.

Be so one with me that nothing, absolutely nothing else
        matters.

Your parents may die, the stars may fall,

Yet nothing can separate us.

This is all that matters

Yesterday I took you upon my lap.

I took away your cares.

I tucked each one into my pockets.

Do not sneak them back.

Live today in the fullness of love;

Do not be concerned about tomorrow
for I hold all you tomorrows in the palm
of my hand.

I give you to my mother.

Her tender compassionate love will heal you.

She is like the woman with the ointment.

She was not afraid to risk because she loved.

Keep loving, keep giving, keep risking—

I am with you.

My peace is calming the inner core of your being.

My Spirit will carry you to the Father
if you but trust me with all your heart.

My Mother will show you the way;
she is your unfailing star.

*I am your
Good Shepherd;
I bring you
oneness,
oneness with me,
oneness with others,
oneness with nature.*

I go gently among you,
as gentle as a flower.

Hope for Religious Life

"Listen to my voice; then I will be your God and you shall be my people. Walk in all the ways that I command you, so that you may prosper."

Jer. 7:23

Know the unearthly strength, the unending love,
        the constant hope of waiting on my spirit.
Be aware that the wind of my Spirit
        is blowing through your community.
Know that I am changing you, all of you,
        slowly,
        peacefully,
        almost imperceptibly.
I go gently among you. I call you to be
        of one heart
        and one mind,
        one faith,
        one corporate thrust.
I am your Good Shepherd.
I do in you what you can't do in yourself:
        I bring you oneness—
                oneness with me,
                oneness with yourselves,
                oneness with others,
                oneness with nature,

> oneness with the pope,
> oneness with the male, chauvinistic church,
> oneness with the starving in Africa,
> oneness with the thirsty in Basutoland.

My Spirit is sweeping through your community.

You must let her.

You must be as open as the sky and as true
> as a fresh mountain stream

You must continue to let my love in you go out
> to all in need.

Never stop loving.

This earth is thirsty for love,
> yawning, aching, ever reaching out for my message,
> fresh and new and life-giving.

My dear fireballs, let me lead you.

Trust me and step out boldly.

Use the fine gifts I have given you to settle cares about
> land use, cars, finance, housing, ministry,
> health, reformation, apostolate.

Come to me often.

Remember there is NOTHING TOO BIG FOR ME to
> manage.

Trust me and relax for your Father loves you
> and I carry that love daily to Him in the Eucharist.

To a Busy Principal Who Tried to Do Too Much

"My help is from the LORD who made heaven and earth."

Ps. 121:2

O my struggling one,

My power in you has not been vain.

Let me recharge your batteries.

You struggle and try too hard.

You don't let me act in you.

Be still long enough for me to act.

I can

and will,

      but you must let me.

You can't do it all by yourself.

Commit your life to me and I will act in you.

O child of constant activity,

Let me be your activity.

Trust me with all your burdens

and I will carry them effortlessly.

You tend to carry the whole world

      on your shoulders.

It is my world. Give it back to me.

I came to bring you life,

       not this heavy burden

       which you insist upon.

Let go and let me.

I know the way to the Father.

I know the way past all these trumped-up burdens.

Put your hand in mine and praise the Father.

Your were made for praise,

       not to be weighed down with cares.

To One Who Tends to Run Away

"Christ's peace must reign in your hearts, since
as members of the one body you have been called to that
peace. Dedicate yourselves to thankfulness."   *Col. 3:15*

My dearest one,

Let my light shine upon you.

Do not be afraid, do not run away.
>   My light is hope,
>   My light is truth,
>   My light is oneness.

Let my light fill your life.

Walk in the peace of my light
>   that you may know me
>   in new and deeper ways.

Let my River of Love inundate you.

Know the peace that comes from saying "Yes"
>   to all the Father asks.

Know the joy of living and loving in my Presence.

Feel the caress of my Mother's lips upon your brow
>   as she takes away your fear and
>   fills you with the good gifts of my
>   Father.

Child of tall concerns, let not your heart be troubled,

I see your needs—I will answer.

I have given you the capacity for love.

Do not let this frighten you.

It is my love, it is my heart that I have given you;
I will be responsible for it.

All you need to do is to say "Yes"
        and put your hand in mine
        as I put my heart in you.

Child of fearful running, I am with you.

I am taking away your fright and giving you
        what you must desire—
        the ability for unlimited love,
        the love of my heart,
        the love that has loved this world
        even to the end,
        and still loves it now.

Come let my love in you pour out.

Let your heart be broken for others as mine was.

This is the gift I ask of you.

Dearest one, you run, but I catch up with you.

You fear, but my love casts out all fear.

Relax and let the strength of my love do in you
        what you cannot do in yourself.

Praise me, child of trembling knees

and let my love come through!

To a Nun Concerned About Many Things

"Do not let your hearts be troubled,
have faith in God and faith in me." *John 14:1*

Walk in my truth.

Walk in my beauty.

Walk in my love.

Know the great peace
  that comes from being in my Presence.

Do not ask for the moon—

I give you not only the moon, but the sun and stars
  as well.

Before the stars burned bright,

Before the whales spouted,

I called you by name, I loved you.

I planted wisdom in your heart.

Nourish that wisdom and continue to let her reign
  supreme in your life.

Walk with wisdom.

Talk with wisdom.

Pray with wisdom.

Relax with wisdom.

Let your whole being be inundated in wisdom,
  for wisdom is my Spirit flowing through you
  like an endless river.

Wisdom is my love preparing you for a new work.

Be patient with wisdom and be patient with yourself.

My Spirit works gently, oh so imperceptibly.

Lay aside the past and let the gentle balm of my Spirit

     make you new.

I alone am your god, your Shekinah glory,

     your hope, your new beginning.

I judge only by the heart.

If your heart is in me and beats one with mine,

     nothing else matters.

I am healing the worry crevices you insist on.

I do not need money, I only need your heart.

All the money in the world is as chaff to me.

Do what you can to help your community

     but do not be hung up on money.

Walk peacefully through this world.

Use only what you need.

Share everything I give you,

     and you will live in my love.

My love is more precious than all the shekels

     in the world.

I have made your heart for love,

     not to worry about money.

Listen to your superiors,

      but do not be unduly concerned about finance.

My will for you is peace.

I want your heart set on higher things.

Endeavor to please me,

      walking in my beauty and truth.

Rejoice in my love

      for it is more precious

      than anything this world can offer.

Integration

"Of you my heart speaks; you my glance seeks;
your presence, O Lord, I seek."   *Ps. 27:8*

Come to the fountain of living water.
Rest there and know the great comfort
    my Mother sends you
    through the power of my death on the cross.
Liberate yourself from all vain, evil, or distracting
    thoughts.
Free your heart and your mind to rest in me.
Love me with every atom of your being.
Trust yourself to my loving care.
Do not be concerned about little things,
    pleasing this one or that one.
Please me and know that I dwell in you,.
The water that I give is living water.
It shall become a fountain within you,
    leaping up to provide eternal life.

Understand that I am
    your bruised reed,
    your smoking flax.
Do not crush me in the poor and rejected.

Chapter 4
Fruits of Peace

*I let a flower
bloom, I never
force it.*

To a Person Searching

"Let us discern for ourselves what is right; let us learn
between us what is good."   *Job 34:4*

Come to me.
Know that I am your perfect fulfillment.
Do not walk in a desert of your own making.
Know me in all that happens to you.
Love me in the valleys and rough terrain.
My hand is over you. I have never let you walk alone.

Do not be discouraged.
Do not be anxious.
Let my anointing pour through you.
Know that you can't do it by yourself
But know that in me all things are possible.
I have called you to life and laughter.
My perfect design for you is peace.
You will know my peace in ways you never dreamed of
If you open your heart to the will of my Father.

Come.

Walk with me.

Trust me to act in you.

Like Lazarus I will unbind you from the shackles
        of this earth.

I will open your eyes to the delights of my Father. You will
        know me in a new way

And your heart will dance in the presence of your God.

Drink
my peace;
eat my peace.

I plant wisdom
and truth in the gentle
earth of peace. This
is where they flourish
like a dandelion

Peace as a Cornerstone

"...my peace is my gift to you; I do not give it to you as the world gives peace."
John 14:27

Come to me
    and let me unravel your woes.
Let me speak to your innermost heart
    that you might know
    the great peace to which I have called you.
Be at home with all that is unsettled in you,
    all that is jarred,
    all that is jagged,
    all that is un-peaceful.
My will for you is peace.
Drink my peace,
Eat my peace,
Breathe my peace.
Hold fast to my peace for it is my beginning gift.
Upon it all the others rest.
Let my peace fill you and go out to all those
    with whom you work.
Realize anew that my peace is the starting point
    for your ministry.
Nothing can grow in ferment and hurry,
    anxiety and worry,
    unrest and duress.
I plant wisdom and truth in the gentle earth of peace.
This is where they flourish, like a dandelion.
Let your heart be peaceful and all my gifts can grow.

Truth

I felt God was saying:

O my child,
Do not be afraid to speak out.
You must be truthful with yourself and with Arlene.
The principle of the thing is wrong.
Be gentle but be truthful.
I am with you, I will guide you.
Do not be afraid.
Nothing on this earth has the power
      to hurt you in such a way
      that my love cannot heal it.
I have commanded you to speak the truth;
Do not run away from it.
My peace will come after the storm.
You must trust me with all your heart
      and accept this responsibility.
I am with you all the way.
Take the risk of what might happen to you
      and do not turn back.
Trust me.
I have seen you through much bigger things.
MY LOVE IS BIGGER THAN YOU CAN EVEN IMAGINE.

Be calm.

Be at peace.

Be confident that my Spirit will guide you.

You have sought me and I am with you.

Cast aside all your doubts, your fears, your worries.

Know that I want only your good
      and Arlene's good.

I am your tower of strength.

My Spirit of truth will speak out.

My plans are like a spring flower coming up gently. . .

Patience

"They that hope in the Lord will renew their strength,... They will run and not grow weary, walk and not grow faint." *Is 40:31*

You tend to be impatient.
Wait upon me quietly,
      lovingly,
      trustingly,
      peacefully,
      prayerfully.
I am doing all things.
Don't rush.
My plans are like a spring flower
      coming up gently,
      responding patiently
      to spring sunshine and rain.
You tend to want everything on the spot.
Little one,
I don't work that way.
My plans are one with my Father
And as such they unfold gradually.
You must have the eyes of faith.
My ways are not your ways,
My plans are not your plans.
Be patient, let my plans bear fruit.
Any forced growth will not be of me.

I let a flower bloom—I never force it.

If you are of me, you will never force things.

My Spirit blows where he will.

My plans for you are perfect and complete.

Let me unfold them; don't yank them out of my hands.

I will share them with you; just don't be
      so impatient.

You Americans want an acorn to be an oak overnight
      and if it doesn't happen
      according to your specifications,
      you heap up a plastic oak tree
      and pretend it's real.

Let my word come alive;

Place no counterfeit in the way.

I am a God of truth and integrity.

So please do not spoil my work
      with your American sense
      of consumerism.

I say to you today let my word unfold slowly.

I am not a God of haste.

I build in the slow cycles of the seasons.

I build in truth, I build in realness.

Sham, and silly counterfeit is not for me.

You are a people of much haste.
>   You rush,
>   You grab,
>   You push,
>   You shove.

You want instant coffee and instant success.

I say to you:
>   Calm down.
>   Sit still
>   Know your real nature.
>   Feel the rhythm of the seasons.
>   Know the inner stillness of your
>   own heart where I reside.
>   Let me be your God.

>   Make your heart quiet
>   and open for my message.

How can I deliver it if you are
>   perpetually jumping around
>   like grasshoppers?

I need quiet.

I need your full attention.

I need carefully tilled soil
>   in which I can plant seeds
>   of truth—my plans
>   for your future.

Give me what I ask, and you shall know the glory
>   of the Lord.

*I build in the slow
cycles of the seasons.*

Freedom

"Show me the way in which I should walk for to you I lift
up my soul."   *Ps. 143:8*

With tenderness and compassion,
with graciousness and love,
I have called you to go forth and heal others.

Give of me as never before.
Step out in love.
Step our in truth.
Step out in hope.
Let me be your River of Life.

Know me in the depths of your heart.
Know me in the depths of trial.
Know me in the depths of struggle.
Know me in all that happens to you.
Love me in all that happens to you.
My goodness will never drop you.
My strength will see you through.
My hope will restore you.
My kindness will mellow you.
My peace will inundate you.
You will know me in new and deeper ways.

You will walk with me and talk to me
in all that happens to you.

You will embrace me with the freedom
born on the cross.

You will understand that to be nailed
is to be free.

My spirit will wash you in your own tears.

Renewed and restored you will help others.

You will share my healing love.

Your life will have a new dimension of praise.

You will glorify my Father in the unending love
of my Spirit.

You will know no act, no word, no joy, no hurt, no sorrow
too small to praise me.

You will come to me often with open arms and a hungry heart.

You will let me fill you with all the good things
my Father has in store for you.

Wisdom

"Resplendent and unfading is Wisdom, and she is
readily perceived by those who love her, and
found by those who seek her."   *Wisdom. 6:12*

O my people,

I give you wisdom,

I give you peace.

Accept my peace.

Hug my wisdom.

Love to share all I have given you.

Turn to me with grateful hearts.

Recognize the gifts of my Father.

Know my wisdom and you will live.

Know my peace and you will rest.

Know my heart and you will love.

You will share the wisdom and love I have

          poured into you.

You will change my world.

You will let the beauty of my wisdom touch it.

See how unending are the fruits of this Gift!

Sharing

"And he led forth his people with joy; with shouts of joy, his chosen ones."

Ps. 105:43

O my people,
I come to bless you by this sharing.
I do not ask for the impossible.
I only ask that you speak
 in truth and simplicity.
Do not run away from what I plant in your heart.
Water it and come before me
 singing for joy
 and carrying your sheaves
 to be shared
 at the market place
 of others' hearts.

I fill you with the good things of my Father,
 hope and truth,
 beauty and goodness.
Do not be afraid to share.

Freely have you received,
Freely give.

Freedom from Tension

"You will show me the path to life, fullness of joys
in your presence, the delight at your right hand
forever."   *Ps. 16:11*

Beloved,
Go down deep into your inner being.
Rest with me.
Take a deep breath and let all the tension out.
Feel the quiet beat of my love.
Listen to my heart.
Put away your brain.
Set it on the shelf with your glasses.

Find me in everything,
      in the golden flowers,
      in the deep blue larkspurs,
      in the friendly farmer,
      in the wild roses,
      in the birds' twitter,
      in the sleek, black skunk,
      in Helen's gentle ways,
      in the fresh cantaloupe,
      in all that is and will be.

Find me, for I am there, waiting for you.

I caress you in every breeze.

I love you in every tree.

I delight you in every cloud.

I revitalize every atom of your being.

Come to me on the swift feet of hinds

and let me refresh you with the living water.

Know me in every sound,

     in every word,

     in every footfall.

Know me and love me, for I am bursting the bounds

     of creation

And I long to be one with you!

Giving

"You need to recall the words of the Lord Jesus
himself, who said, 'There is more happiness in
giving than receiving'."   *Acts 20:35*

"Be hanged if I'm going to do one more thing for Joan," I
sputtered to my friend Arlene. "Look, I got her all she needed for
her special project and, when I asked her to pick up my medicine
order, would she? 'No, I don't have time'."

I was angry. Being generous didn't pay. But the Lord had
other ideas. He spoke firmly but gently:

I have poured out myself in love to you.

> Give,

> Give with your whole heart.

> Give as never before.

Let my spirit have complete reign in your heart.

Detach yourself from all this world offers.

> Let my Spirit fill you.

> I am enough for you.

> Go out to others.

> Never stop giving.

> To live is to give.

My life in you is the source of giving.

> Give when you are happy.

> Give when you are sad.

Give when you are angry,
      resentful,
      upset,
      puzzled,
      joyous,
      charged with the grime of the past.

Give, O my beloved, give your whole self
Let no person,
      no thing, no event, no pussycat
      or otherwise, stop you from giving.
You were meant to give freely, lovingly
      with no strings attached.
Give the most to the ones who hurt the most.
This I ask of you. This is the way I want you
      to grow in my love.
Discipline your life that my giving might be
      present in you.
My Spirit will speak through your giving.

Chapter 5
Family Life

*I only ask
for the continual
giving of your hearts
as family.*

Love is a
flower opening
ever wider
in the sunshine
of life.

To a Bride

"...the fruit of the spirit is love..."   *Gal. 5:22*

My Child,
I have called you to union with Mike.
Let my heart beat in you as
    my love draws you ever closer together.
Love is a flower opening ever wider
    in the sunshine of life.

Cherish love.
Remember love is patient, love is kind,
    love never fails to give.
Love holds no grudges.
Love is my spirit in you.
Love is ever-giving as my spirit is giving.

As you grow in life and love
    do not be afraid of pain.
Love grows through pain and through joy.
Love is my most precious gift to you
    in this month of May.
Come apart
And know the fullness of my love for you
    in your love for each other.

Rejoice in that love and go forth as husband and wife,

> one in heart and mind,

> one in spirit,

> one in hope,

> one in the strength I will give you.

I have called you by name to be one.

Come, rejoice!
For this is the day I have made for you.

Cana Couple

"On the third day there was a wedding at Cana
in Galilee and, the mother of Jesus was there."   *John 2:1*

Al and Marsha are a beautiful couple who were on the same
prayer-group pastoral team as I was. We got to know each other on
a faith level. We prayed Al through his Bar exams and Marsha
through her first pregnancy. Early in their marriage, Jesus assured
them:

My beautiful couple,
>   I am with you.
>   I desire your togetherness.
>   As I am one with my church, so you are one
>   with each other.

>   My love and my goodness will fill your hearts
>   TOGETHER.
>   Let there be that oneness in you that was in me
>   as I strove on earth to do my Father's will.

>   I made you two one that you might glorify me.
>   Glorify me in the love of my Spirit.
>   Praise me in hearts full of gratitude.
>   Know me in new and mysterious ways
>   as you pray together
>   And let your little ones join you,
>   for I am the author of life
>   and I desire new depths of life for you.

Synchronize all events of your two lives
      into one great song of praise.
      Come together as husband and wife
      and child of grace,
      and little one yet to come,
      and praise me,

For I desire your praises as a family.

I am with you in all things.
      I love you and
      I do not ask for impossible things.

I only ask for the continual giving of your hearts
      as family.

My love is strong.

My love is all-encompassing.

My love desires oneness,
      oneness in me and
      oneness in each other,
      oneness with the little one
         I have given you and
      oneness with the new life
         I am giving you.

Do not hassle,

Do not struggle;

Just quietly take the ordinary means to be one
      in me and in each other—

a loving greeting,
a wee prayer,
a child's game,
a simple meal,
a nice outing,
a shared puzzle.

I only ask of you simple things as a family.
You don't need to reform the world.
You just need to let my love run freely
among you,
between you,
and around you.

How?

Just a word,
a gesture,
a smile,
a kiss,
a hug,
a gentle forgiveness—

Just those simple things I enjoyed
as I grew up in Nazareth.

I don't ask for tax reforms
or world-shaking events;

I ask only for the ordinary done with my heart
of love.

I ask of you great joy and contentment
in my life in each of you,
a prayerful quiet witness

that I live among you,
that my gentle, unceasing love
is flowing like a river
in your happy home,
that I am there
in the ordinary and the obvious.

I am among the pots and pans.

I am in a child's tears and laughter.

I am in the unborn's heartbeat.

I am in the attorney's office.
Nowhere am I not.
Everywhere am I.

Look to me for I am with you
and that oneness which is my Spirit
will flow between you
as peacefully and gently
as the July breezes,
and as joyfully unconscious
as the air you breathe.

I am your life; live in me as I do in you.

Know me with the full intensity of your hearts.

Love me with every atom of your being.

Let the full vitality of my love fill your lives.

To a New Mother

"May the Lord increase you and make you overflow
with my love for one another and for all, even as our
love does for you."   *Thes. 3:12*

O child of new life,
I am with you.
Know that nothing can happen to you
        without my Presence.
You are not alone.
My goodness shall follow you all the days of your life.
I cradle your baby in my arms.
I breathe life and love into this small child.

You will know me in this small life.
You will find my beauty reflected here
        in a very tangible way.
Look to me and I will restore your energy.
I will give you new vigor.

I am the Lord your God.
I hold you in the palm of my hand.
I have created you and your child,
        your family and your husband.
I will not drop any of them.
I love you with a love beyond telling.

I remove your burdens.

I fill your life with love.

Let nothing on earth keep you from me.

Give me your tiredness,

     your blues,

     your aching muscles.

I made you and I understand the chemistry of your body.

Give me all that weighs you down.

Know the great joy I have in store for you!

Jesus Speaks to a Wife and Mother of Nine

"As the Father has loved me, so have I loved you.

Live on in my love." *John 15:9*

Margaret was very much in love with Jesus. She was also a devoted wife and mother of nine. She had serious heart surgery, triple by-pass. It didn't work right. She had to have a second surgery. She got better, but she wanted to join Jesus. She felt guilty for wanting to join Jesus because her youngest was only thirteen; but she wanted it so badly, Jesus took her.

Seek me quietly and peacefully in your daily duties.

I am there,

My love is welling up in you,

> like an eternal fountain.

> Let my love wash away anything that is not of me,

> any word,

> and thought,

> any action

> that does not bring you to the Father.

Yes, let my love wash it away.

I am a lover, strong and gentle.

I seek the totality of your being.

> Give!

> Give!

> Give!

Give with a heart free and loving!
Give with a heart that seeks only the fullness
        of my Father.

O child of much yearning, you desire union.
You desire me in the bosom of my Trinity.
You have reached out and tasted divinity,
        and nothing on earth can satisfy you.
This taste is my gift.
Cherish it, but be patient for I cannot yet take you
        to that endless circle of Praise
        which is my Trinity.
You must stay on earth and do my Father's will.
You must be a good wife and mother.
You must nurture your children in my love.
You must lift all things up to me.
Know that I work through the daily stuff of living.
I am with you in a most intimate way in the
        most mundane things—
        cooking,
        cleaning,
        shopping,
        listening to teens,
        working with a drunk.

I am there.

My peace will touch all.

Come, beloved.

Share the gift I have given you, compassionate love
    and desire to do my Father's will.

You need not run to the ends of the earth.

SHARE MY LOVE RIGHT WHERE YOU ARE.

Give of me in each daily incident.

Be Eucharist to all.

Let those who touch you touch me.

This is my will, that you let the oneness
    I have with you
    go out to others.

Come, give me your heart
    and I will give you mine in return.

I will let the love which beat for you on Calvary
    beat for all those you touch.

O my beloved,
    in solitude and deep prayer
    my Father's Will will be revealed to you.

You will discover daily new ways
    to love me and
    to let my love go out to others.

Shalom, little one, my peace is in you. Call on my peace when life gets bumpy

More Problems

"Do not be saddened this day, for rejoicing in the Lord must be your strength."   *Neh. 8:10*

Jane was married and had eight children. When she became pregnant with the ninth, she was very surprised. She wasn't planning another and felt guilty because she really didn't want it, but she didn't want the child to feel unwanted. "It's just that I already have so many children," she explained. Also, she didn't believe in abortion. She felt stuck. She prayed. God heard her.

O little one,

     bearing life within

Rest in me and I will support you.

Know the strength of my love in these days ahead.

Do not be burdened.

Do not be saddened.

Understand that your lack of physical strength

     is normal at this time.

Seek me with all your heart.

Welcome the new life within you.

Trust me to support you

     in all that this new life entails.

I am your God and I know you through and through.

My will for you is peace.

Lean on me in your husband.

Keep entrusting all your children to my care.
Sleep with a good conscience
> knowing you have done and are doing
> all you can to help your children
> stay close to me.
Pray often with your husband
> for the spiritual growth of your family
> and then just hand them over to me.
I love you, Jane, and I will never abandon you.
You are faithful to me—
I will always be faithful to you.
My love and my grace will not leave you
> in time of need.
Let my love in you speak easily, peacefully, quietly
> to your family.
So do not be disheartened at your own shortcomings.
I allow these so that you might see that you need me.

Shalom, little one, my peace is in you.
Call on my peace when things get bumpy.

To a Lady Caught in Jealousy

"We know that God makes all things work together for the good of those who have been called according to his decree." *Rom. 8:28*

O my daughter,

My love calls you to be yourself.

Do not run away from your problems.

I am there;

I will not abandon you.

My strong arms are around you.

Do not be afraid of your faults, your sins,

      your imperfections.

My love can and will work through them.

Consider Paul's "I boast of my weakness.

      God's power in me is made perfect in my weakness."

Your anger, your frustration, your jealousy

      are all means of letting me work in you.

Do not be afraid of these things.

Give them to me.

When you first feel angry or jealous, say,

      "Jesus, help me" and I will.

I am there to help you.

My love is real.

It is not just for those moments
       when you are happily smelling the violets.
It is for those rough moments when you feel alone,
       overburdened,
       afraid,
       jealous,
       hurting.
I AM WITH YOU.
Know that little Billy is the tangible love
       between you and your husband.
Share his beauty and goodness.

Don't be afraid to share what is deepest and truest
       in you—my love.
Talk to your husband.
Tell him your frustrations, your anger, your jealousy.
Let my love in him heal you.
Pray together.
Listen to my Spirit in you as you pray together.
I will never let you down.

My Living Water will
set you free of this
blackness which casts
such a dark shadow
on all your relationships.

More Jealousy

"May he enlighten your innermost vision that you might know the great hope to which he has called you, the wealth of his glorious heritage to be distributed among the members of the church, and the immeasurable scope of his power in us who believe."

Eph. 1:18-19

My child of inside rocks,

Let me dissolve all that is hard within you.

I see your blackest needs,

I know your inner struggles.

I am reaching out to save you from yourself.

    Let me.

Do not be consumed by darkness,

Do not let jealousy weigh you down.

Give me your jealousy,

Trust me to heal in you all those raw ends
    that jangle your nerves.

Stop comparing yourself to your sister.

Jealousy comes from trying to grab other's gifts.

Look at my gifts in you,
    Love and use these.

Lean on your husband.

Trust the great love he has for you.

Let my blood wash you free of jealousy—
    free of this pain in you,
    free from what his might do
        to those you love.

Let my Living water set you free,
    free of this blackness
        which casts such a dark shadow
        on all your relationships.
My will for you is peace.

My will for you is freedom.

This freedom will come about by your letting go
        of this jealousy that is
        eating you up.

    You can't wash it away,

    But my love can and will if you let it.

Be your best self by loving and accepting my gifts
    In your sister and in you!

To a Mother
Whose Daughter Was in a
Serious Car Accident

I felt Jesus was saying:
> No one can come to the Father except through me.

Little one, resting in the lap of the Father,

Know that my strong love is with you.

Know that I come to you in this terrible event
> of your life.

Yes, I am with you in hectic planning, I am with you
> in prayer-filled plans.

I touch your being with the gifts of my Spirit—
> love,

> joy,

> and hope.

Let these three fill your nights and your days.

Give your daughter to me.

Know that my goodness will fill her life.

Do not be anxious.

All things works to good for those who love.

My love has followed you, Judith.

I am a tireless lover, my love knows no bounds,

My love knows no barriers.

Give me your heart—your heart was made for giving
And you will know me in the giving.

      Give freely.

      Love fully.

Have concern for what happens around you.

      I am there.

      I am in the midst of it.

My Presence will pursue you.

I thirst for your love.

      Rejoice.

      Give.

      Love.

And know deep down in your heart
That I am healing your daughter.

To a Friend
Whose Brother Was Dying of Cancer

"We do not lose heart, because our inner being
is renewed each day even though our body is being
destroyed at the same time."   *2 Cor. 4:16*

My faithful one,
Lay your weary head upon my shoulder
And I will give you rest.
Come to me and let my love and life revive you.
Let me take the cares off your shoulders.
Do not worry about Bruce,
For I hold him in the palm if my hand.
I see his needs, I know his heart.
My gentle love covers him like a warm blanket.

You are faithful, child of the Father.
My goodness touches your life.
My goodness in you touches
        all those with whom you work.
Have confidence. I will give you strength
        to do all you need to do.
My goodness is a strong lamp in your life.
It gives light to all those about.
Never stop leaning on me.

I am with you, I go before you always.

Praise me in all that is and will be.

Trust your brother and your mother to me

and to the tender love of my Mother.

She will never leave you.

She presents your concerns to my heavenly Father,

And I always bend my ear to listen to you.

Rejoice.

Hang loose.

Love me in every moment.

I am yours forever,

and my love is the beginning of eternity.

My love is the strong light of goodness in you.

Share it.

Glorify me in sharing my goodness.

My goodness shall follow you all the days of your life.

You will know me in new and deeper ways.

You will love me with a love born of my Spirit.

Rejoice! for I have called you to be one with me

that all you do is done in me.

To a Mother
Worried About a Son in Trouble

"Those whom the LORD has ransomed will return..." *Isa. 35:10*

O my troubled one,

I am with you.

I desire peace for you.

My Spirit will lead you.

My Spirit will guide you.

Come to me with all that weighs you down.

I long to lift this weight from you.

I see the desires of your heart.

I, too, desire goodness for your son.

Do not give up.

Keep coming to me in prayer

    and I will not abandon you.

Trust me with all your heart.

Love me in every situation,

    even in this black one.

Remember that in me all is possible.

My power in unlimited.

By yourself you can do nothing;

    in me you can do all things.

Give me this care and all the others,

For I will carry them to the Father
> who has promised:
> Ask and you shall receive.

Ask in my Name, O child of worry,
And I will answer.
I will show you how to untangle this mess.
I will order all things in peace and hope.

You must trust me and keep on praying.
Do not be afraid.
> Reach out in love to this child.
> Be firm,
> Be fair,
> Be a listening parent.
> Know what he is saying.
> Give him the security and strength
>> of your strong love.
> And know that I am with you through it all.

To a Family in Dissension

"I have set before you life and death, the blessing and the curse. Choose life, then, that you and your descendants may live, by loving the LORD your God, heeding his voice, and holding fast to him. For that will mean life for you..."   *Deut. 30:19*

Know that my love is stronger than any bonds
>of fear,

>of anger,

>or misunderstanding.

Turn to me in deep prayer and know that my love in you
>will do the healing.

Trust me as never before.

I am the Center of your family.

I can bring good out of past mistakes.
>Apply love, not reason.

>Apply peace, not logic.

>Apply understanding,
>>not I-told-you-so.

Lay your intellect aside and let my spirit in you
>do the acting.

You are the waterpipe; I am the Living Water.

Let my life run through you to give life.

My Spirit breathes where he will.

You must follow him and never enclose him
in your intellect.
He cannot be bound. He is freedom itself.
He is life, and peace, and unity.
Let my Spirit heal all that is troubled in your family.

To an Elderly Lady
Who Lost Her Husband

"The Lord was moved with pity upon seeing her and said to her, 'Do not cry'."
Luke 7:13

O my daughter,
Grieve not.
Your beloved is with you in spirit.
And I am with you in spirit.
I will take away your sadness.
I will touch your heart
  with the beauty and goodness
  of your beloved.
I will never leave you alone.
My strength will support you.
My love and goodness is waiting for you
  like an endless reservoir.
Come, drink deeply.
Know the great peace that awaits you
  at the fountain of my delights.

Walk in spirit around that beautiful lake
  you enjoyed with your husband.
Be aware that he is very much with you.
Be aware that he is sending you his best.

Understand that his heart is one with yours.
Speak to him and
speak to me
and
feel
the
oneness of our spirits.

Taste the joy that will be yours
When together
We will praise
Your Trinity.

Realize that I can
work through the
thorns of yesterday
and bring you to the
joy of today

Chapter 6
Healing

My
love is
big enough
to heal the
past and to
call you to
a future
full of hope.

Healing

"One day Jesus was teaching, and the power of the Lord made him heal."   *Luke 5:17*

"He heals the brokenhearted,
and binds up their wounds."   *Ps. 147:3*

Child of pain,
I go before you in steadfast love.
I want you to rest your cares in me.
I am your living Bread.
I will feed you.
I will heal you.
I will guide you.
Know that my love was poured out for you
        on the cross.
Know that I care enough to give all.

Stop running away from your imperfections,
        your sins,
        your shortcomings.
Realize that I can work through all of these.
Realize I do work through all of these.
O child of stress,
I can handle it.

Trust me.

There was no time when I wasn't with you.

When you had a bad childhood experience,

I was there.

When the dog bit you in the arm

I was there.

I never left you for a moment.

I saw your pain;

My heart was sad.

I reached out to help you.

I never stopped until the pain was gone.

Now you understand pain and hurt.

Go out and help others.

Show them my healing love.

Go forth and witness forever.

In peace and love you will love me.

Use all gently for in the very torrent

of passion

You must acquire and beget a temperance

That will give all your actions smoothness.

Don't rush at things.

Go gently, beloved,

My Spirit is a gentle Spirit.

Don't push.

My Spirit is never pushy.

Just rest quietly

and drink deeply

at my Fountain of Life.

My love is washing gentleness and tenderness

into your life,

That you may go and share it with others.

I am filling you with the good things of my Father

That you may give as yonder myrtle gives,

never asking a return,

never pulling back—just

quietly,

gently,

steadily,

deliciously giving.

TO GIVE IS TO LIVE AND LIFE IS MY BEST GIFT.

Realize that I can work

through the thorns of yesterday

And bring you to the joy of today.

Help in Time of Trouble

"God indeed is my savior; I am confident and unafraid.
My strength and courage is the LORD, and he has been
my savior."

Is. 12:2

My friend, Sister Arlene, a city person, was named to be
principal of a rural school. She had never been a principal. She was
afraid. I tried to support her. We prayed together. It seemed as if
God were showing us Arlene on a huge combine. Tiny 98-pound
Arlene was running this monstrous machine all by herself. We
laughed at the Lord's sense of humor and continued our walk along
the edge of a lush corn field. Then, as we continued to pray, the
Lord assured us that he could remove any obstacles.

Why are you cast down? Why to you fear?
Don't you know that I am with you?
Lift up your head. Lift up your heart.
Be confident that I am your answer in this time
of trouble.

I am with you. I have never left you alone.
You feel alone. You feel obstacles bigger than
your ability to cope.
That is good for it brings you to me.
My love and my grace are sufficient for you.
I long to gather you in my arms and tell you

The harvest is great
and you are the laborer
I have chosen.

MY POWER IS MADE PERFECT IN YOUR WEAKNESS.

I have placed you here and given you a work to do
that I ask of no other.

It is yours to do. With my help you will do it.

Trust me as never before.

The harvest is great, and you are the laborer
I have chosen.

Run my reaper with confidence;

My hand is over you.

My heart beats one with you.

My strength will be your strength, and I will supply
what is lacking.

Turn to me and know that the energy of my spirit
will take complete charge.

My spirit will guide your machine

And in the process you will know my Father.

You will come to Him with a heart full of love,

And He will take away all your cares.

My Father will make your machine a vehicle of faith.

He will supply you with all the courage you need
in this time of trouble.

Courage

"Be brave and steadfast; have no fear of dread of them,
for it is the LORD, your God, who marches with you; he
will never fail you or forsake you."   *Deut. 31:6-8*

Mark was twenty-six years old and had been addicted to hard
drugs for a number of years. Three times he had been through
rehab centers, but to no avail. Then Jesus helped him out of a
death-threatening situation. He came to our prayer center and told
us that it was only the Lord who got him off drugs. He asked us to
pray with him. We did. This is what Jesus said:

My son,

Though you walk through a dark valley,

You shall know no fear,

For I am with you.

My love and my strength will support you.

Do not dwell on the past.

When it comes up to frighten or disquiet you,

Give it to me gently, peacefully, lovingly.

I am your all.

My strong arms are around you.

Know that my spirit is within you.

Know that I can conquer any darkness.

Let not hour heart be troubled,

Nor let it be afraid.

I am with you through it all.

My love is stronger that all the powers

of darkness.

Call on me often, for I am with you

And I will see you through.

There is no evil,

no darkness,

bigger than I can handle.

Trust me with all that is still hurting in you,

all that is at unrest,

and know that I will fill you

with hope.

Come, strong son of my Father,

put your hand in mine

and together we will go forward.

You have nothing to fear

For I will pick you up as tenderly as a mother;

I will love you into wholeness.

Have courage—

I am with you now and always.

Problems

"Yet he knows my way; if he proved me, I should
come forth as gold."   *Job 23:10*

Anne is a career lady. She is single and has worked for years
for a large insurance company. She is an expert in her field, but her
boss is impossible, overbearing, critical, jealous, and very difficult
to work with. Anne came for prayer, feeling lower than the tail on a
mole.

O my child,

O my daughter of much worry,

Come to me and lay your burden at my feet.

Know that I can work through

      all that is festering,

      all that is troublesome.

Know that my spirit in you can bring order

      our of chaos.

Know that my healing Spirit can mend

      bad relationships.

You must stay open to me

      and I will act.

You must sit down and talk to your boss.

You must see where he is coming from.

You must understand, if possible,

his point of view.

I am guiding your relationships,

Be at peace.

Walk slowly in the way of mending these problems.

Let my Spirit in you run over abundantly

in good deeds

and loving service.

Smile with the joy of my Trinity.

Love with the deep love of my Mother.

Hope with the same hope I had on the cross,

hurting, yet always turning

to the Father.

Bless with the power of my Spirit in you.

Praise with every atom of your being

For I am the Lord your God

And you shall have no other.

Give me that situation that drives you crazy.

Know me in these rough spots for I am there

And I never cease helping you.

Negative Feelings

"And this hope will not leave us disappointed
because the love of God has been poured out in our hearts
through the Holy Spirit who has been given to us."

Rom. 5:5

You are angry, resentful
    bitter,
    distressed,
    uneasy,
    ready to do a murder.
Negative feelings are choking you.
I understand.
I am with you.
I see your needs better than you see yourself.
I long to free you from yourself and all that
    weighs you down.
Give me your anger, your resentment.
Give me all that is unresolved and uneasy in you.
Give it to me daily.
Know that you cannot do in yourself
    what needs none.
Know that I can and will.
Do not submerge your feelings.

Out of the black soil
of today grow the white
lillies of tomorrow.

They will only crop out in wrong ways that
    embarrass you.
Own your feelings, both good and bad.
Give them to me, both pleasant and unpleasant.
Trust me to heal in you the root causes—
That little child who wasn't loved enough.
Know that my tender love is always there.
Know that I long to give you that freedom
    that comes from trust.

Be patient with yourself and forgive yourself.

Life's Hurts

"For a tree there is hope, if it is cut down,
that it will sprout again, and that its tender
shoots will not cease."   *Job 14:7*

There is no hurt so big I can't fill it.
There is no pain so deep I can't heal it.
> Come,
> Drink my living water
> That you may know my healing love.

> Come,
> Let all that has been torn asunder in you
> Be put together in me.
Know the beautiful power of my healing love
And let it embrace you.

Rejoice!
Out of adversity will come fresh strength.
Out of sorrow will come new beginnings.
Out of emptiness will come new life.
All this is possible in me.

Remember—

Out of darkness of the tomb

    Came the light of my Resurrection.

Out of the black soil of today

    Grow the white lilies of tomorrow.

It hurts to love with my love.

But when you respond with my love,

    You will be set free,

    And you will come closer to me.

You will know a healing

    That this earth cannot give.

Come, and let my love heal all that is hurting.

Rejection

"We do not lose heart, because our inner being
is renewed each day . . ."   *2 Cor. 4:16*

Give me your past.

Give me your rejection.

Give me your loneliness.

Remember—

I was there when your family rejected you.

I saw your pain when your own father put you out.

I will touch your innermost being with peace.

I will transform the pain and hurts of the past.

Listen to my Spirit in your friend.

Show her the places that are hurting.

Speak the truth in a spirit of love.

Then my love can heal you.

I long to take away this load
  you have carried for so long.

I long to fill you with hope
  that is eternal.

My love is big enough to heal the past
  and to call you to a future
   full of hope.

Rejoice!

For this day I have begotten you anew in my love.

You must be free of all
this rubbish, as free as
a dandelion in the breeze.

Freedom to give

I felt Jesus was saying:

"I will dwell with you and walk among you,
I will be your God and you shall be my people."

I can free you from your own hang-ups.
>   Trust me.
>   Trust me no matter what.

I prepare your heart for new life like spring plowing.

The time of planting is at hand.

Come let the seeds of faith blossom into love.
>   Do not be afraid.
>   Do not condemn yourself.
>   Seek me with a peaceful heart.

I make all things new.

I sprinkle clean water upon you.

I give you a new heart.

Do not run away from my gifts.

Use your sensitivity to help others.

Turn your eyes upon me.

I will show you the blessedness of the Father.

I will do a new thing in you and you will live.

You will be prepared to give as never before.

You will be blessed by the very things
>   that weigh you down.
>   You will learn what I teach
>   from the inside out.

My Spirit in you will transform you.

My power is made perfect in your weakness.

Open your heart and receive
                    the love which is yours.
          Stop running away.
          I tire of chasing you.

I long to set you free that you might give
                    the good gifts
                         my Father has for you.
          To give hope you must trust.
          To give peace, you must be peaceful.
          To give healing, you must be healed.
          To give love, you must experience my love.
          To give me, you must be one with me.
This is what I ask—do it and you shall live.

Know from the depths of your innermost being
          There is no gift worth giving save me.

I come in many ways—open your heart, your mind,
                    your hands, your whole being
          To the wonder of my love
          that you may know how to give me and only me.

Tears wasted on your own past,

Untimely digging, morose brooding—

None of this is of me.
          Let it be gone.
          Have none of it.
          Reject rejection—
          It has no place in my ministry.

Humbly ask others to help you,
          To deliver you from your own hang-ups
          That you may be ready for my work.

You must be free of all this rubbish—

As free as a dandelion in the breeze.

The first wisdom I
will give you
    is the wisdom of
    forgiveness,
    of letting go completely
    of washing yourself
    in the blood of the Lamb.

Forgiveness

"If you bring your gift to the altar and there recall that your brother has anything against you, leave your gift at the altar, go first to be reconciled with your brother, and then come and offer your gift."

Matt. 5:23-24

My child,

ever reaching out,

searching,

thirsting,

struggling,

I am with you.

My nailed hands will show you how to forgive.

Reach out with love to all those who hurt you.

Sincerely ask forgiveness of all those you have hurt.

My forgiveness runs free and deep in you.

Do not be afraid to utilize the power of my Spirit
in you.

Do not be afraid to initiate forgiveness.

I am with you,

I see your weakness—

I will be your strength.

From the cross I will show you what forgiving love is.

Love gives all and asks no return.

You keep asking the return of justice.

You must leave justice to my heavenly Father.

Mercy is my domain;

Justice belongs to my Father.

You have asked for wisdom.

The first wisdom I will give you

      is the wisdom of forgiveness,

      of letting go completely,

      of washing yourself

      in the blood of the lamb.

Accept my forgiving love and let it wash you free
      of your starched righteousness.

I am loving forgiveness.

I extend my mercy to all.

If you want to be forgiven
      You must forgive completely.

Then with open hands and a renewed heart
      You will stand before me,
      And I will teach you the wisdom of the Spirit.

I will teach you how to praise and glorify our Trinity
      even in pain.

You will walk in my ways for I will take your hand

And I will show you what delight it is
      to join that endless circle of love
      which is our Trinity.

How to Unscramble a Relationship

"When the hour comes, you will be given what
you are to say. You yourselves will not be the
speakers; the Spirit of your Father will be
speaking on you."   *Matt. 10:19-20*

My beloved worrywart,
I am with you. You do not like what you see
      in the scrambled relationship
      with your sister.
Be patient—I am healing it.
Go out in love, stop judging her.
Know that I love her just as she is—
      messy housekeeper,
      sloppy,
      tardy, etc.
Look at her good points,
And stop playing "Miss Perfect."
I love you where you are.
Can't you do the same for her?
See how lovingly she cares for your mother.
Stop looking at the stuff on the floor.
And see where true values are.
Take time to sit at my feet and learn

where true values are.

Take time to sit at my feet and learn
  to see with my eyes.

I have loved life into you.

You must love life into her.

If you did but know the gift of my living water,
  you would not get hung-up on trifles.

You have this time to enjoy
  the full circle of love of our Trinity.

Praise me and let me carry you to the Father
  on the wings of my Spirit.

Praise me even in the relationship
  that is not all it should be.

Go back and see the layers of hurt your sister
  has suffered from being the spoiled youngest.

Let my Mother's heart of understanding beat in you
  that you might judge your sister only in love.

Love is the only healing there is.

Stop throwing bricks and learn to love.

Let the love I have for you go out to her.

Wear your faults patiently,
  for it is through them that I draw you
  to the Father in the forgiveness of the Spirit.

Unity and Forgiveness

"Pardon, and you will be pardoned."   *Luke 6:37*

"If you bring your gift to the altar and there recall that your brother has anything against you, leave your gift at the altar, go first to be reconciled with your brother, and then come and offer your gift."   *Matt. 5:23-24*

Anger made my chest tight. That principal had no right to yell at me in front of 32 students. It wasn't fair. It wasn't right. Why should I forgive her? I hadn't done anything wrong. She was uptight. It was her problem. Then the Lord spoke to me through one of my friends.

I have called you to witness to me.

Speak out.

Know that I am the Lord your God.

Speak my message in a spirit of love.

Gather all people to me

And let there be oneness among you.

If there is hatred, or anger, or resentment,
        among you,

Get that healed first.

I cannot work in you when your heart is set
        against your brother.

I have come to bring peace and a spirit of oneness.

In unity is your strength.

Heal the divisions among you.

Don't be afraid to humble yourselves
And make peace with your brothers.

I am the peace flowing between you.
My heart in you will make you heart beat as one
      with your brothers.
Go out in love.
Let there be no division or pulling apart.
I desire oneness before sacrifice.

I have come that you may have life,
And to have life you must be one with me,
      and one with each other.
Let my healing love break down any barriers.

Jesus Speaks on the Means to Union

"You need to recall the words of the Lord Jesus himself, who said 'There in more happiness in giving than receiving'." Acts 20:35

The deeper our union, the more I ask of you.

Love gives all.

Love never counts,
>   never pauses,
>   never doubts,
>   never wonders,
>   never questions,
>   never measures.

Love just gives and gives and wants to give more.

Love cannot find enough to give.

I seek your whole heart.

You still try to protect yourself too much.

You run away when things get too hard.

You are afraid to give me your emotions.

Trust me to help you in this area.

Do not be so proud.

Cry if you must, but give me your tears.

I gave my life for you—you must give yours for me.

I made you as you are—accept yourself

And give according to your means.

I love you as you are.

I believe in the goodness of my creation.

I call you to deeper union through every facet of life.

Chapter 7
Discipline

Remember:
the greatest
penance is
the denial of
self-concern.

Necessity of Penance

"I wish to know Christ and the power flowing from
his resurrection; likewise to know how to share in
his sufferings by being formed in the pattern of
his death."

Phil. 3:10

My struggling one,
You see with the eyes of faith what I am asking you.
You must be willing to walk peacefully in the desert.
> You must give me your wayward emotions.
> It will not be easy.
> If you really love me,
> You must give here as never before.
> I showed you in prayer what I meant.
> Now it is up to you.
> To let yourself be vulnerable is not your style,
> > but I do not ask you to do it for me.
> It hurts and it takes a lot of giving.
> You see clearly how it takes a deeper love
> > to do this.
> Physical mortifications are good,
> > but they are not enough.
> They are only the tot's beginning prayer,
> > a necessary step but very small.

Do not omit them.

Today your eyes are open—you see what I ask.

DO IT.

And never forget what the good Padre told you

so long ago:

THE GREATEST PENANCE

IS THE DENIAL OF SELF-CONCERN.

Forget yourself, and don't be concerned

whether or not

people will like you.

Be reasonable and forget yourself.

The minute you begin to center on yourself

give it to me.

It does not please me when you worry about yourself.

Your time belongs to me.

Give me the penance of not being overly concerned

about yourself.

I love you, my child,

And I seek your whole heart.

Give me all.

I made you as you are.

I love you—nothing more is needed.

Cast all your cares on me, for I have care of you.

Discipline

"He therefore let you be afflicted with hunger, and
then fed you with manna, a food unknown to you and
your fathers, in order to show you that not by bread
alone does man live, but by every word that comes
forth from the mouth of the LORD."   *Deut. 8:3*

I have called you to discipline.
Discipline your body
      that my spirit might speak through you.
You can't do it by yourself,
      but I can do it in you.
I can show you how to discipline your body
      so that my Spirit in you will be set free.
Listen, for I am speaking to your heart.
My words are real, my words are light—
      do not neglect them
Listen carefully.
I beseech you to know me from the inside.
I will restore your body,
      but you must follow carefully the diet I give you.
You must eat according to my design,
      not your whims.

You are my vessel of election;

      I have called you to wholeness and happiness.

In order to hear me and let my light come through

      you must rid yourself of excess weight.

You much cannot do this by yourself,

      but through my power all things are possible.

Come, put your hand in mine and trust

      that I can and will do it in you.

Eat only what you need.

Enjoy your food.

Eat slowly.

Eat sanely.

Eat to glorify me, not your tummy.

Come, glorify me in all you do

      whether it be

      eating of drinking,

      sleeping of praising,

      walking or working.

*I am your Bread of Life;
feed on me and you will
never hunger.*

Jesus Speaks on Overweight

"Whatever came to be in him found life."   *John 1:4*

I have come that you may have life
     and may have it to the full.
My life is a discipline of love,
       not the rigid kind that does not allow
       room to breathe, but a gentle, quiet discipline,
       a peaceful love that puts all things into
       perspective and calls for trust in the loving
       care of my Father.
You are eating too much.
Eat less, and you will have life, my life.
Discipline your body that my Spirit might speak
     through you.
Trust me to do in you all that needs done.
       Eat to live—don't live to eat.
I come in quiet order.
Peace is the tranquility of my order.
My peace will flow through you
       if you have the courage to discipline your
       eating habits.

I am your Bread of Life.

Feed on me and you will never hunger.

Know the love of my spirit and you will be satisfied.

You will not want food you don't need.

Live in me as I live in you.

Know me in everything that happens to you

      and you will know life, my life.

Get rid of all the excess around your waistline.

It is totally uncalled for, excess baggage.

Let me show you how to rid yourself

      of this adipose tissue.

My Spirit will guide you in the correct way

      of eating, but you must be open.

Praise me in this sacrifice of love.

Come joyfully before me, eating only what you need.

Letting God In and Leaning on Him

"My help is from the LORD who made heaven and earth."

Ps. 121:2

Do not look down on anyone,

Look to me and see the good in all.

This is what I ask of you.

Mortify your senses.

You failed badly today.

Yesterday was fine, but today was out of line.

My love,

My peace,

My hope

> will grow in you
>
> if you are faithful
>
> to what my Spirit says to you.

My love is rich;

My love is deep;

My love is overflowing in you.

You will not always feel sensible consolation.

I ask this of you because I love you.

Can you return that love?

Tonight for the first time
      you really let go
      and leaned on me.
You are beginning to understand
      what I am asking.

Open your hands.
Open your heart.
Open your life to my love.
I desire to fill you to the fullest,
      but first
      you must let me in.

Chapter 8
Mission

you are called to have a ministering mentality: open, caring, compassionate...

Finding God in the Marketplace

"I assure you, as often as you did it for one of my least
brothers, you did it for me."   *Matt 25:40*

Long have I waited for you in the marketplace.
Long has my heart reached out to take your heart into mine.
Love me in all the daily events of living.
Know me in every raindrop.
Find me in every person, young or old,
Love with the power of my Holy Spirit.
Let go of all those things in you that are struggling.
Give them to me with a peaceful heart and united spirit
        for I am there.
I have never left you.
I desire to teach you the prayer of the marketplace.
        Love gives,
        Love bends,
        Love is wherever I am.
Be at ease in praying in turmoil and confusion.
Do not be afraid to let my love in you spring forth
        to bless all those around.
I am with you, and I desire to share the depths and
        richness of my love.
I will show you how—you need not hassle.
Just love me with all your heart and give me every moment.

*Love me in
every facet
of life,
in the falling
rain, the
bright flowers...*

Ministering Mentality

"The gift you have received, give as a gift."   *Matt 10:8*

You are called to enlarge your tent, your life, your heart,
    so that I might increase the scope of my work in you.

You are called to have a ministering mentality,
    open, caring, loving, giving, compassionate,
    careful to respect the fragility of each person,
    gentle as my Mother is,
    gracious as your foundress.

You are called to be yourself in a world
    that is sometimes busy trying to make you everything
    but yourself.

You are called to share my life.

Wear your faults patiently and know that you have come
    quickest to me through your own brokenness.

Love me in every facet of life,
    in the turning leaves, the falling rain,
    the brilliant sun, the bright flowers,
    the intense communion,
    the ugly remark, the dragging tiredness.

Love me for I am there and I call you to deeper life.

I call you to wholeness that you might share my heart in you
    beating for all my people, crying out for the
    transformation of my Trinity in this world, so hungry
    for the justice of my Father.

I call you to share all that is good and beautiful and true,
    for this is the way I will transform my world.

Jesus Speaks on Mission

"Then I heard the voice of the LORD saying, 'Whom shall I send?' ... 'Here I am,' I said; 'send me'." *Is. 6:8*

"My Father is at work until now, and I am at work as well."

John 5:17

Go in peace,

    my hope,

    my love,

    my truth.

Step out boldly and carry my message.

    You are my hands.

    You are my feet.

    You are my voice.

    You are my heart.

Let my love pulse through you and go out

    to others.

Touch them, and I shall live.

Minister to them, and I shall walk.

Fill them, and I shall no longer be hungry.

Trust me to act in you.

Be confident.

Still your nervous breathing.

Let my spirit do my work.

Trust me with all your heart and
> you shall live.

I have a mission for you.

I would send you forth,

But first you must be stripped clean
> of any resentments,
>
> any shadows,
>
> any grudges,
>
> any fears.

My Spirit cannot work
> when you put up a road block.

BE FREE IN ME!

Give me your resentments, your grudges, your fears
> and know that my heart is big enough
>> to handle them all
>
> and to prepare you for the mission I have in
>> mind.

Ministry

"It was the Lord who did this and we find it marvelous to behold."

Matt. 21:42

Do not be afraid to be poured out in loving service.

The heart was made for giving, to barter all the earth.

Let your heart be broken and given for me.

Let nothing come between us.

Let all you do build up my Body—

    Let my strength be your strength.

    Let my forgiveness be your forgiveness.

    Let my love be your love.

Remember, there is nothing you cannot do in me.

I am your source, your powerhouse.

Come to me and know life.

Let my life so fill you that you will be able to share,

    To be poured out in loving giving.

Be aware that before you can help others

    You must trust the pruning power of my love.

    You must let me fashion your heart after mine.

    You must accept your faults and wear them patiently.

After you do these things, you will find

    that my will for you is loving service.

I have anointed you with the power of my Spirit

    To minister to my people,

    Those cast aside, those rejected,

    the suffering, the little ones.

I have gifted you—I have sent you forth

    To live with my heart,

    To bless with my hands,

    To speak with my lips.

Give in my name.

I have loved life into you—

    Love life into others.

Remember, when you are weak, I am strong.

    When you are helpless, I am

powerful.

    When you can't, I can.

Minister to my people as my Spirit directs you.

Apostolate

"Go... make disciples of all nations.
Baptize them in the name of the Father,
and of the Son and of the Holy Spirit."   *Matt. 28:19*

I am training you.
I am fashioning you.
I desire you to do my will.
My people are hungry.
My people are thirsty for the things of God.
My Church is in ruins from too much structure.
My people are not being fed.
I have commissioned you to feed them
My Spirit will show you how.
Only my Spirit can satisfy this hunger and thirst.
You must listen carefully as I form you
        for this new mission.
I spent thirty years preparing for mine.
You must be very patient with my priests.
After three years even my Apostles did not understand.
You must love my priests and help them grow in me.
I have come that you may have life and may have it
        to the full.
My Spirit gives life.

You must give my Spirit to my priests.

Then they will live.

Accept the pain they give you as an offering of oblation.

In pain you will learn to love.

Do not be afraid of pain for pain can be very redemptive.

I came not to do away with pain but to fill it with meaning.

I love you and I am fashioning you for this new work.

Trust me and walk in faith.

Knowing that I am with you through it all.

You will see a dark tunnel.

Do not be afraid to walk through

For I am with you though you perceive me not.

My Spirit is with my Church.

I will raise up leaders

And I will give the leaven to what needs changing,

To free us of dead, lifeless structure,

To keep what is sound, to save the timbers that hold
    the cross beam.

Trust me and continue your walk in faith.

Mission

> "All this I tell you that my joy may be yours
> and your joy may be complete."   *John 15:11*

Go, be my healing love. Go, be my hope
>   in a world that has many hopeless scenes.
Go, be my heart
>   to a people that are often heartless.
Go, be my hands
>   for a people entangled in things of earth.
Go, be my Spirit
>   for a spiritless people.
Go, O best beloved of my Father,
>   for my power will overshadow you,
>   my heart will beat in you,
>   my words will tickle your brain,
>   my message will pour out of your mouth.
Go, be at peace for I am with you
My message is a strong message wanting to be heard
Wanting to be lived, wanting to be given in love
With all the graciousness my Father has poured into you
Through my Spirit.
O best beloved, enjoy these rare moments and
>   be willing to share.

Chapter 9
Mary

Open
your-
self
to Mary
and she
will fill
you with
my Spirit

Jesus Speaks of His Mother

Know that my Mother has a special love for you.
Know that her tender concern will help you
       in your darkest moments.
She will share her strength
       her joy,
       her hope,
       born of saying "Yes" to my spirit
       working in her.
You will find a new dimension of loving in Mary.
Open yourself to her and she will fill you
       with my Spirit.
Her warmth,
Her beauty,
Her openness
       will fill your life
       with a power for goodness
       you have never dreamed of.
O little one of many fears,
       trust me
       and my beautiful Mother.

I am your Good
Shepherd; I will
guide you peacefully
through your director
and through my Mother.

Original
wood carving
by author

Magnify the Lord
with Mary and you
will have life.

Mary

"No, the water I give shall become a fountain within him
leaping up to provide eternal life.   *John 4:14*

Turn confidently to my Mother.
She is your safe refuge in every storm.
She will bring you safely home.
Trust her and let her form me in you.
Be patient with yourself.
Accept your limitations, your idios, your faults.
I work through them to bring us closer together.
Your faults are the gateway to compassion.
Seeing yourself not perfect, you will be
         less inclined to jump your neighbor.

Praise me in your faults and know they are
         a means of deeper love and union.
I want your heart.
Forget all the trivia and come to me.
Find me in the NOW.
Trust my word in your director.
I have gifted your through my Spirit.
Listen carefully and follow—I am your Good Shepherd.

I will lead you peacefully through your director

    and through my Mother.

Come today to my Mother.

Place yourself and all you are in her hands.

She is a loving Mother.

She knows your inner being—she sees your needs.

She is motherly enough to care for all of life.

Nothing is too small for my Mother to nourish.

She will nourish you too.

You must go to her without any reservations.

Her spirit will breathe in you if you but ask her.

    Her spirit is my Spirit.

    Her ways are my ways.

    Her life is my life.

When you say "Mary," she says "Jesus."

Turn your heart over to Mary,

    and she will bring you to me.

She is a perfect channel of my love,

    my truth,

    my hope.

She is that gentle peace that surrounds my Trinity.

Join her in praising my Trinity

For here is where life begins!

Mary, Mother of Forgiveness

"When you stand to pray, forgive anyone against whom
you have grievance so that your heavenly Father may
in turn forgive your faults."   *Mark 11:25*

Come,
Ask my Mother for a peaceful heart,
        that you might have the insight and discernment
        to root out all those things
        which spoil your relationships with your
        companions and with our Trinity.
My Mother is loving and has a tender concern for you.
She has guided you from your youngest years—
        she will not fail you now.
Come to Mary and let her show you
        the path you must walk.
She listened to my Spirit and will show you
        how to do the same.

My loving kindness is bigger than life.
Let my loving kindness wash away
        your guilt,
        your fears,
        your anger,
        your undue concerns.

Then run to Mary and, with her, praise my Trinity.

It is here that you must rest.

It is here that you must live.

It is here that all your desires will be met.

To share in that endless love of our Trinity
      is the beginning of life.

I have come that you might have life
      and might have it more abundantly.

Let that life in you, my Spirit, praise the Father
      through the joy of Mary.

Magnify the Lord with Mary and you will have life.

You will know what it is to forgive.

You will know how to accept forgiveness.

You will be free—my Word will make you free.

MY LOVE WILL FREE YOU TO BE YOURSELF.

Come rejoice with me,

For I see the desires of your heart,
      and I will honor them.

Remain open and I will fill you with my gifts.

Remain docile and I will wash you free
      of all that is not of me.

Go often to my Mother and seek her counsel,
      for her heart was wounded but forgiving
      and she will show you my ways.

Giving Like Mary

"As the Father has loved me, so I have loved you.
Live on in my love." *John 15:9*

I will uncling you from the things of this earth.
I will show you how to fill your heart
　　　with the things of heaven.
You must come aside to my mountain
　　　and let my beauty break your heart.
You must not be afraid to be pouring out in giving.
In giving you will be closest to me.

Ask my Mother.
She understood giving as no other mortal has.
She let her heart be broken again and again
　　　because she loved me.
She understood pain.
She was not afraid to embrace pain.
She knew pain was a means, not an end.
She knew that pain could be the path to the Father.
She knew that I was with her all the way.
She trusted completely and was not afraid
　　　to walk the path my Spirit showed her.
You, too, must walk that path.
You must let my river of love wash you free
　　　or your faults and fears,
　　　your sins and shortcomings.
It can and will.
In me the fullness of the Father's will is made known.
Praise my Father in the ever-flowing stream
　　　which is my Spirit.

Mary's Umbrella of Hope

"Dismiss all anxiety from your minds. Present your needs
to God in every form of prayer..."   *Phil. 4:6*

Do not argue—
Do not fuss.
Look to me in love and hope.
Let my Mother cover you
            with her umbrella of hope.
Forget not my benefits.
You do nothing alone.

Come to me, little one.
Come to me and let me replenish you.
My stores are unlimited.
I am holding all you need.
My Mother longs to satisfy
            your every need.
Come,
            let my Mother be for you
            new hope.

Reincarnational Love

"For he who finds me finds life,
and wins favor from the LORD."   *Prov. 8:35*

My truth in you is deep—do not be afraid.
All the Father has is mine,
    and all I have is yours for the asking.
Consecrate yourself to truth—let my Spirit grow in you.
Speak my truth in a spirit of love.
My truth in you will continue to set you free.
You will know each day the reincarnation of my love.
My love in you has not been void.
This love will spring in completeness where my feet pass.
You will know the freshness, the wonder, the power
    of my Incarnational love.
It will bring forth my truth in you to be shared.

Let the power of my name continue to fall
    on every part of your life.
Remember—he who finds me finds life.
The power of my name is your life
    in all those grubby situations.
Bless me.
Praise me.

Love me in all that happens to you.

Remember—I am closer to you than your own heartbeat
      and I am drawing you deeper into that
      full circle of love—my Trinity.

In me you live and breathe and move and have your being.

Let me bring you to the oneness, the beauty, the depths
      of our love community.

My heart beats with yours—let yours beat one
      with the Father
      in the free flowing love of my Spirit.

You have found Him whom your heart loves—
      take hold of him and do not let him go.

Walk with my Mother, talk with my Mother.

Confide your mother to mine.

Let her be for you the great sea of peace
      in which our Trinity rests.

In her is the fullness of me.

In you she is calling forth my reincarnation.

Of my fullness you have received, love following upon love.

Let that love tickle your toes and carry you
      straight to the Father.

Let that love be your guiding force

And let the peace which is my Spirit
      fill every atom of your being.

Chapter 10
Love, Joy, Union

I have shown you
the mountains where
your love will be one
with mine.

God's Love

"And this hope will not leave us disappointed because the
love of God has been poured out in our hearts through the
Holy Spirit who has been given to us."   *Rom. 5:5*

"I pray that you may have your roots and foundations in love.
So together with all God's people you may have the power to
understand how broad and long and high and deep is Christ's love.
Yes, may you come to know his love although it can never be fully
known and so be completely filled with the perfect fullness of
God."   *Eph. 3:17*

I have placed a seal on your brow
> that you may admit no other.
>> Be mine.
>> I am yours.
>> I love you with a love bigger than you
>>> can measure.

O my beloved,
Let me feel the caress of your lips.
Let me know the touch of your hand.
Let me hear the sound of your voice.
Your heart was made for me and you will find your rest
> in my arms.

Come to me.

I long to fill you with life,

      the life that is my Spirit.

Nestle safely in my arms

      and know no fear.

My love will support you.

My hope will sustain you.

Be aware that you will be broken to feed others.

Understand that it is in being broken

      that new life is given.

Like the wheat in the earth

      you must die to give life, my life.

I have carried you in my heart—

I will not drop you.

I have loved you with a love big enough to write

      in blood.

Recognize the power of that love and respond

      with every atom of your being.

*Look
and you will
see traces of
my love in
every leaf,
in every
raindrop...*

Take all the beauty and goodness of my creation and let it bring you to me.

God's Presence

"... acquire a fresh, spiritual way of thinking." *Eph. 4:23*

"Who will separate us from the love of Christ?
Trial, or distress, or persecution, or hunger,
or nakedness, or the sword?" *Rom. 8:35*

I was sitting in our little chapel praying. Sunlight was streaming in. A single pink rose stood by the golden tabernacle. God's peace touched me, and he said:

> Take the sunshine of today
>
> > and let it bring you closer to me.
>
> Take all the beauty and goodness of my creation
>
> > and let it bring you to me.
>
> Let the violets and roses I put in your path
>
> > praise me.

> Take the pain of today
>
> > and let it bring you closer to me.
>
> Do not spurn pain—do not shun it,
>
> > use it to come to me.
>
> Be so one with me that nothing,
>
> > absolutely nothing, can separate you from me.

Look and you will see the traces of my love

> in every leaf,

> in every child,

> in every raindrop.

I am speaking to your heart

> in all that is and will be.

>> Look

>> and listen,

>> taste

>> and smell

>> and you will find

>> what your heart desires most—

>> the fullness of me.

In the dew of little things your soul will find me.

Jesus Speaks on Little Things

Find me in everything.
      Accept the little things that turn you off
           with a graciousness born of my love.
In the dew of little things
      your soul will find its refreshment.
      There is nothing small
           in the service of God.

        A small note,
        A hearty handshake,
        A package carried,
        A smile given—
These are the little things my heart asks of you.

Give and never stop to count the cost.
Give as only one can whose heart is wrapped in mine.

*I am the vine; you are
the branches*

Jesus Speaks of God's Life

"I am the vine, you are the branches. He who lives in me
and I in him, will produce abundantly."   *John 15:5*

I am with you—have no fear.
        Come to me in confidence and love.

I will show you the way to the Father.
        Trust all your works to me;

I will imbue them with life.

I will make them fruitful.

I am the vine; you are the branches.

Stay one with me
        that the life of my Father
        may flow through you
        in the love of my Spirit.

Have great confidence
        in the power
        of my unending love.

I am with you,
        I see your needs,
        I will never let you down.

Rest in the warm embrace
        of my love.

Know me
        in a strong and gentle way

for I am with you

to guide your every thought and action.

My love goes out—my love pours through you.

Know me with a confident heart.

Know that I have come to gather,
to restore, to heal,
to bind up, to put together,
all things in my Father's love.

I have known you in the dawn and in the darkness.

Lean on me with sure confidence, for I carry you in the palm
of my hand.
I will never drop you.
Come to me with a quiet, peaceful heart
and rest in the pleasant shadow
of my love.
Let my love sweep over you,
let my love fill you,
let my love possess you,
let my love consume you
for I am yours and you are mine.
Life here is just a distant horizon—

Life in me is an eternity of bliss.
Know me, beloved, as I know you.
Come, put your hand in mine
and together we will go to the Father,
giving Him unending praise
in that ocean of love,
which is the Trinity.
Come, know the life
to which you are called.

Jesus Speaks God's Love

Know that my love for you will never end.

     Before the sun burned bright,

     Before the rivers flowed,

     Before the mountains sat in place,

     Before the birds sang,

          I called you by name!

          I called you to be my own.

I love you—do not be afraid.

Love me by giving all.

Do not cling to anything on earth—

     Not family,

     Not friends,

     Not jobs,

     Not real estate,

     Not clothes,

     Not houses,

     Not even prayer forms.

        KNOW ME AND ONLY ME

Dispossess yourself of everything

Belong to me with the totality of your whole being.

Know that I am the Lord your God

and you shall have no other.

Know me in the depths,

Know me in pain.

Know me in sickness,

Know me in bubbling joy.

Know me in people,

Know me in the desert.

Know me in the whole of life.

Trust me with the mighty hope

I have planted in you.

Do not rely on people—let go of everything except me.

Give as never before.

I am with you.

I have never left you.

Loosen up and trust me

with a trust that matches my love for you.

O my child, I have loved you with an everlasting love.

With great tenderness I have gathered you

into my arms.

My love for you will never end.

Stillness in God

"Be still and know that I am God: I will be exalted
among the heathen, I will be exalted in the earth."

Ps. 46:10 (KJV)

O my daughter, trust me completely

and snuggle up in my arms

that I might fill you with my choicest gifts.

My love is flowing through you

like an infinite river.

You must go out to others.

Remove all barriers.

Have confidence—I have overcome the world.

You will understand each step of going out

as I unfold it to you.

Do not ask to see everything at once.

All I ask now

is a quiet, peaceful heart,

an acceptance,

a resting in my arms.

When you are completely quiet,

my Spirit can fill you.

When you are completely full of me,

then you can step out and help others.

I cannot mission you forth

    until you stand still, sit still, be still

    long enough for me to fill you

    with wisdom, understanding, counsel,

    knowledge, piety, fortitude, and

    fear of the Lord.

I long to gather you into my arms

    and pour all of these into you

    in the fullness of my love.

As long as you are anxious and concerned

    and busy about many things,

    I cannot do it.

See, O daughter,

    and feel the gigantic bigness of my love.

    All the greatest greats

    are a pale shadow by comparison.

Be still and see for yourself

    that I am the Lord your God

    and my love must consume

    every fiber of your being.

Be still

    and love me with everything that is in you.

You must never lose your
sense of humor. My
Spirit will speak in you
if you remain open to
my joy... the simple joy
of a daisy.

Joy

"They will meet with joy and gladness, sorrow and mourning
will flee." *Isa. 35:10*

Do not strive to figure out ways
   to cope with your own sensitivity.
That is my gift to you. I can work through it.
I work gently and joyfully.
I will work through it,
   but you must come to me in confident love.
Cudgel your brain no more about these things
   because I work through the heart.
I speak inside, deep-down things.
I am not a surface God.
I am not in intricate schemes.
I come in small ways, in quiet peace.
I always speak in the language of your heart, love.
I desire totality in giving—I desire complete dependence
   on me.
You can't do it by yourself.
KNOW ME IN ALL THAT HAPPENS TO YOU.
   LOVE ME IN ALL THAT HAPPENS TO YOU
   through the actions of men and angels,
   yourself included.

I love you with a love more vast than the Pacific,
    more encompassing than outer space.
I will never forsake you—even if your father and mother
    forsake you, I won't.
I will be there in season and out.
You can always count no me.

With tenderness and compassion I have called you
    to bind up my hurting member.
You must be my heart.
You must give joyfully.
You must share the life I have poured into you.
You must bind all things up gently
    in the hope my
    spirit gives you.
Go, tell it on the mountain—
Go, tell it on the prairie:
    My message is light, my message is peace.
You must be my light and peace—
    You must be my hope and laughter.
Let my joy echo and re-echo in your life.
You must never lose your sense of humor.
My spirit will speak in you
    if you remain open to my joy.

A Song

"My lover speaks; he says to me, 'Arise, my beloved, my beautiful one, and come! For see, the winter is past, the rains are over and gone. The flowers appear on the earth, the time of pruning the vines has come, and the song of the dove is heard in our land'."

Song of Solomon 2 :10-12

Beloved,
You are my song
that fills my heart.
Sing it.
Do no drag it.
Sing me.
Carry me joyfully.
Share me peacefully.

Use EVERYTHING AS A MEANS OF LOVING ME.
Take all the negatives,
All the frustrations,
All the inside-out, upside-down things
that happen as a result
of your humanity
or those around you
And use them to love me,
Use them to bring others to me.
Power is made perfect in weakness.

I am most there when you feel me the least.

My love can work in the darkest corners of the tomb.
My love can shine out in the night
more readily visible
than in the noon day sun.

A Deeper Drink

"All you who are thirsty, come to the water! ...Come without paying and without cost,..."

Isa. 55:1

My child,

My love for you never grows weary, never grows old.

It is as fresh and vital as the day I called you forth.

It is as rich and alive as the creamy white flowers

> of spring.

It is as close as the air you breathe.

It is as real as the smile of your sister.

Rest in that love, drink in that love,

> trust in that love.

Let me hold you in the curve of my arm

> and daily fill you with the power of my love

> that you might step forth and love others,

> unafraid of the darkness where no one has trod,

> knowing that you must trust me with all your heart

> and open yourself to the gentle power of my love

> in others.

I come in all people—do not shrink back.

DRINK DEEPLY OF HUMANITY

> AND I WILL SHOW YOU THE FULLNESS OF ME!

Paradox of God's Love

"Yet if we love one another, God dwells in us,
and his love is brought to perfection in us.
The way we know if we remain in him and he
in us is that he has given us of his Spirit."   *1 John 4:12-13*

My beloved,
I have led you out of the desert, into the oasis
     prepared by my Mother.
Come to the banquet and feast on the good things I have set
     before you.
My Father asks for a sacrifice of love.
You were willing to go where he led.
He is pleased with your gift and now asks
     that you be seated at his banquet.
Rejoice in the peace which is the first gift of my Spirit.
     SWIM DELICIOUSLY FREE IN THE GREAT LOVE
     MY FATHER HAS FOR YOU.

Bask in the River of Hope which is Mary.
Walk peacefully.
All we ask of you has the full support of our Spirit.
You will know great sorrow, but our joy will fill you.

You will walk in darkness, but our light
     will illuminate you.
You will struggle with pain, but our love will fill it
     with meaning.
You will taste ashes, but our hope will bring new life
     out of the ashes.

See, we are doing something new!
Now it springs forth—do you not perceive it!
We have made a new way in the desert,
     water in the wasteland.
Our Spirit is always bringing new life to a torn world.
Have confidence—you will experience it.
Trust and obey.
Commit your life totally to me, and I will act in you.
I will love you with the same love I love the Father.
I will pour out my Spirit upon you and you will grow
     in my ways.
You will experience newness you never dreamed of.
Yes, come to the Father
     in the renewing fire of my Spirit.

Living Water

"Of his fullness we have all had a share,
love following upon love."   *John 1:16*

Come, my beloved.

Come, come, come,

Come to the living waters springing within you.

Come, let my living waters fill you,
      anoint you,
      wash you,
      free you,
      strengthen you,
      renew you.

Come, let my living waters free you
      from the cares of this world
      that you may rest in the bosom of my Father.

Come, let all the love that is my Spirit
      turn you to the face of my Father.

Come aside and know the great love I have for you.

Come let my living waters sparkle deep within
      and show you the face of my Father.

Come, O daughter of much searching and ardent desires,
      rest in me and know eternal life.

Let my Mother caress you—let her turn you to me.

Let her show you the radiance of our Trinity.

She is the peace that surrounds my living water.

She is the perfect "Yes" of my Father.

Know her, my daughter, and you will become one with us.

O Child of love, O child of longing,
  belong to me as I belong to the Father
  through the perfect love of the Spirit.

Praise me in all that happens to you.

Rejoice even in your failings
  for through them I bring you to me.

Know me and you will know the River of Life,
  springing up, leaping up within you
  to praise the Father.

You will know a power and a peace
  that no person can take from you.

Live in my Spirit as my Spirit lives in you.

Come, my love, my dove, my beautiful one,
  do not hide in the cleft of the rocks
  of your own making.

Come to me, bounding over the hills,
  leaping like a gazelle,
  knowing the power and bounce of my love.

Come to me and drink deeply of my Living Waters
  for I carry you to the Father
  in this great River of Love
  which is my Spirit.

Rejoicing in the Lord

"I rejoiced because they said to me, 'We will go up to
the house of the LORD'." *Ps. 122:1*

I teach you his ways ever so gently,
    ever so peacefully.

I open you like a wild rose
    to the power of my love.

I turn you to the face of my Father
    that you might know eternal life,
    that your heart might rejoice in my Presence
    and that you might go on praising me
    even in your sleep.

Come! Come! Come! I love you.

I fill you full to overflowing
    with the gifts of my Father.

I tickle you with delight.

I take away your distracted heart
    and show you how to keep me
    gently on your heart
    today,
    through the unending love
    of my Spirit.

Rejoice, O daughter,
    for I bring you the fullness
    of my Father's love
    in the joy of my Spirit.

Seeing God's Power

"In him who is the source of my strength
I have strength for everything. . ."   *Phil. 4:13*

I have come to you in the night.
I have touched your spirit with the dew of my love.
I have ignited you with the fire of my Spirit.
I have renewed you—I have called you.
I have loved you into wholeness.
Do not be afraid to share what I have so copiously poured
        into you.
Like a river has by grace been within you.
Use that grace, loosen yourself and share the gifts
        I so freely bestow.
Be at peace and know they are my gifts, they are my doing.
People will understand—you have no need to get anxious.
What I have done in you is not your doing.
Give all glory to me.
DANCE IN MY SPIRIT!
Know the great love that has called you beyond yourself,
        beyond what the world can give.
Taste and see how delightful it is to bask in my love,
        to let my gifts in you come alive.

I am your rock, your fortress, your strong deliverer.

Yesterday I showed you my strength when I set Lois free.

You saw the great power o my name—

you saw my love in action.

Believe for I have opened your eyes.

Continue to see with my eyes, to hear with my ears,

to love with my heart.

Know me in every second of time, in every atom of creation,

in every event that happens,

For I am there

and my power in you is alive!

Before the mountains
with their huge bulk
were formed, I loved
you and called you
by name…

Fullness of God's Love

"I wish to know Christ and the power flowing
from his Resurrection."   *Phil. 3:10*

My beloved,
My love has been poured upon you like an unending torrent.
Let my love fill your every pore.
Let my love saturate your entire being.
Let my love inundate every fiber in you.
Remain in me as I remain in you.
Trust my love to fill those dark cracks of your being.

Before the moon was hung,
Before the mountains with their huge bulk were formed,
Before the rivers flowed,
I loved you and called you by name.
I have loved life and goodness into you.
Go now and love life and goodness into all those I put
         in your path—the rejected, the social outcasts,
         the ones no one wants to be bothered with.
Love them in my name.
Minister to them, seeing only me.

I have called you and empowered you to do this.

Do not be afraid.

Step out boldly, knowing my light in you
    will show you the way.

Have confidence. I have shared my heart with you
    and you will share it with these, the least ones.

You will let my spirit in you praise the Father
    at all times.

You will rejoice in the endless love of my Trinity.

Your heart will sing although your body is aching and sore.

You will know me and the fullness of my love
    in the greatest difficulties.

Do not be afraid for I will be with you.

I go before you, child of the Father,
    and the light of my Spirit will show you the way,
    and the love of my Mother will give you peace
    and comfort.

Union

I found Him whom my heart loves.

I took hold of Him and would not let Him go.

He led me among the lilies.

He held me in His arms.

He covered me with kisses and said:

O my beloved,

Be one with me.

Seek me in prayer and you shall find me.

I was with you in the wheat field.

I touched you like a gentle breeze.

I spoke to you through Arlene.

I caressed you in the setting sun.

I have shown you the mountain

      where your love will be one with mine.

Do not hesitate; my arms are open wide.

Respond to my call.

The message is:

Come to the mountain,

Let me Spirit in you pray as never before.

Seek me in the city,

Seek me in the country.

Seek me in the wheat field.

Seek me on the pavement.

Seek me in Arlene

I am there.

But above all, seek me in prayer.

I desire a closer union.

I will cover you with kisses

  And I will show you

  what it is to be one with me.

Relax in my love.

Let your whole being be so filled with me

  that the most painful things

  will be the most precious

  because there you will find me.

I love you, my child,

And I would have your whole heart.

There is nothing too small of too big

  to give me.

Life

"For he who finds me finds life, and wins favor from
the LORD..."

I am your River of Life.

Drink deeply,

Drink often,

And you will know no thirst.

Go

Deep,

Deep

Down

In the quiet coolness.

Let my love wash over you unceasingly.

Let my love still and fill

the core of your being.